Seven Years A Simp

Seven Years A Simp

How I Stopped Simping
And Started Living

By

Chuck Valentine

First edition published by Chuck Valentine June 2021

ISBN (print): 978-0-6452096-0-0
ISBN (eBook): 978-0-6452096-1-7

"Dudes be thirsty as fuck and standards are slipping."

–PAUL JOSEPH WATSON

For my son, L.
And for sons everywhere

CONTENTS

ACKNOWLEDGEMENTS

I'd like to express my gratitude to everyone who contributed, both directly and indirectly, with the writing and publication of this book, in particular Joseph W., who first suggested the idea for the project and provided encouragement and support along the way; and Damien D., whose feedback and editorial expertise proved, as always, extremely valuable. I also owe a debt of gratitude to the many brilliant minds—writers, philosophers, intellectuals and artists—whose insights and ideas have impacted my thinking in a positive way and so too the direction of my life.

INTRODUCTION

Most people today are familiar with the term "simp." In short, a simp is a guy who puts women on a pedestal. So desperately does he desire female attention and approval, he'll do almost anything to try and please a woman, no matter the cost to his dignity.

The term is derived from "simpleton," which is telling with respect to how simps behave towards, and are regarded by, the opposite sex. Simps think little of themselves, making women the focus on their existence. Women, in turn, do not take them seriously. Nor do they want to sleep with them.

The character Lloyd Christmas in the comedy classic *Dumb and Dumber* is the quintessential simp. A limousine driver, he falls in love with Mary Swanson the moment he picks her up from her residence to deliver her to the airport. After she leaves her briefcase at the terminal, he gives up everything to return it to her, driving thousands of miles across the country in the hope she'll be impressed by the gesture and fall in love with him too.

Lloyd, to his credit, at least has the balls to declare his love to Mary. Some simps are so cowardly, so pathetic, that they passively accept the role of "girlfriend with a penis."

Hoping she'll eventually sleep with him and believing himself to be a "nice guy," he does what comes naturally to a simp: he performs favours for her; he listens to her complain about her asshole boyfriend; he likes every one of her *Facebook* posts; he showers her with compliments; and whenever she rants about feminist issues like the "gender pay gap," he nods enthusiastically. Meanwhile, inside of him, anger and frustration build; these shameful, unpleasant emotions he represses.

The simp, like any other red-blooded male, wants to fuck women. More than that, he longs to have meaningful and fulfilling relationships. Unable to obtain the love and intimacy he desires, he resorts to fantasy and escapism. Women become for him golden calves. He whacks off to porn; he drools over tits and ass on *Twitch*; he direct messages women on social media; and, perhaps, if he's feeling bold, he creates a dating profile, only to attract zero dates, or, if he does get dates, to bomb on every single one.

If you're wondering what gives me the authority to write so brazenly on the topic of simping, it's because, for approximately seven years, I was a simp. I sacrificed everything—my identity, dreams, ambition—to try and win the approval and affection of women, becoming a nobody and a nothing in the process. On more than a few occasions, I contemplated suicide. Now a recovering simp, I'm living proof of the damaging impact that simping can have on one's life.

My descent into simping started in adolescence, when I first became attracted to girls—those strange, beautiful, magical creatures who, I felt, were somehow purer and more "spiritual" than members of my own gender. I did little else but fantasise about girls and badly wanted a girlfriend. My crushes were frequent and numerous. But, alas, shyness and insecurity got the better of me. An addiction to porn quickly followed.

When, in my early-twenties, I finally managed to acquire a girlfriend, I was such a hopeless simp that I caved in to her every wish and demand. Though I desperately wanted to leave the relationship on account of her violent mood swings, bullying behaviour and low sexual appetite, I instead went ahead and married her after she repeatedly requested that I do so. After all, I wanted to make her happy and prove what a nice guy I was. And, besides, I was too much of a coward to end things. The thought of being alone terrified me, as did the thought of "abandoning" her and consequently hurting her feelings. Several miserable years later we divorced, at which point she complained that I'd "ruined her life."

What followed, post-divorce, was no better. Just as I'd been a simp with my ex-wife, so I was a simp with the women I dated subsequently. Each one I placed on a pedestal. Each one I tried to make happy, no matter what. Red flags I ignored. My true feelings I swept under the rug. I told myself I was lucky to have a girlfriend, in spite of all the nagging, fighting and drama.

The specifics of these relationships I won't cover here. My years of simping—which, partly for the sake of a decent title, I've counted as seven in total—are laid bare, in detail, in the chapters that follow. All events occurred exactly as described, though some of the names of individuals mentioned have been altered to preserve their anonymity. Where possible, I've added humour, a touch of literary flair, and more than a few sprinklings of philosophical reflection.

It is my hope that, by sharing my journey from simp to strength, it will help others in a similar position find the inspiration and fortitude to choose a better, more fulfilling path in life. Hopefully, too, it will serve as a cautionary tale for those young men who already find themselves battling the temptations of simphood.

As the attack on masculinity continues in the West, propelling us, whether we like it or not, into a female-primary social order, the need for men to support one another, as brothers, can only increase in importance.

1

FRIEND ZONED TO INFINITY & BEYOND

I still remember the words she uttered before kicking me out of her place: "You're not doing it right. I think you should leave."

Words of complete and utter rejection. They haunted me for years, those words. Not just the words themselves, but the bitter, disdainful tone with which she uttered them. Such little worth did I possess in her eyes that, had I been a homeless guy who'd taken a shit on her carpet, she'd still think more highly of me.

I had little to say in response, though I may have laughed awkwardly in a futile attempt to make light of the situation. I still had a boner, but the blood was rapidly returning to my brain. When you've just been brutally rejected by a girl in the middle of finger-banging her, your dick tends to lose its enthusiasm pretty quickly.

After throwing on my clothes, washing my hands in the bathroom sink to remove the pungent odour of wet clam, and grabbing my keys and wallet, I was out the door as quickly as possible. I didn't say goodbye, neither did she.

The journey home was an hour's drive. Worst of all, it was past midnight and I was tired and partly intoxicated. The girl lived in a shitty town in the middle of butt fuck nowhere. Getting to her place earlier in the day had been a mission in itself. Completing the drive home at this ungodly hour required a degree of concentration that I was barely able to sustain. That I was running the risk of being caught drink driving was not unknown to me.

Darkness and rain enveloped me. Trees flashed past like green spectres, illuminated by the high beams of my Toyota. Mine was the only vehicle on the road; I saw no others. The feeling of loneliness was immense.

Self-loathing stabbed at my mind. I was a piece of shit, completely un-fuckable. I'd been rejected by a woman yet again. Usually the rejection occurred early, by means of that awful phrase that no man wants to hear: "Let's just be friends." In this instance, I'd been rejected during the act itself—a first for me. It couldn't get any worse than this. Or could it?

Women rejected me, I realised, because they considered me a joke, a loser, a pushover. I was their "friend," their emotional tampon, their doormat, but never the guy they wanted to fuck. Such men, I knew, are called simps, although I had no idea that *I* was a simp. That realisation would come much later.

I briefly played with the idea of intentionally steering my car into a fence post or a traffic light, erasing myself from existence. People would assume it was an accident, including the girl. Would she feel guilty knowing I'd died on the way home from her place and that she was partly to blame? Unlikely. She had less warmth in her heart than a Taipan.

Her name was Sonia. She was twenty-five. I'd met her at work several months earlier. She had dark hair, large hazel eyes, and a light sprinkling of freckles across her cheeks. Though her face was plain and uninspiring, she made up for it with her physique. She had the greatest ass I'd ever seen—the perfect combination of tight and shapely. It resembled a ripe mango.

On the downside, she was crazy. This wasn't obvious during a brief conversation with her. It was only when she opened up about her religious beliefs or her relationships with guys that the craziness leaked out like noxious fumes. A friend and fellow work colleague told me he knew she was crazy the moment he first looked into her eyes. "Not everything's bolted down properly with that chick," he remarked.

Probably because I was thinking with my one-eyed trouser snake, I foolishly went where other men fear to tread, including those places that weren't "bolted down properly." I should've given Sonia a wide berth, but instead I engaged her in conversation and gradually we started spending time together.

Although still young, already she exhibited all the signs of someone destined to fuck up, over and over again, without learning from their mistakes. I call this the hamster wheel of crazy. But instead of it being a hamster inside, it's a woman, and she's screaming like a banshee and clawing like a cat, desperately trying to escape from the wheel, which only propels her forward even faster.

Women who ride the hamster wheel of crazy both enjoy the experience, because it's exciting and thrilling, and hate it, all at the same time. The fact that it's coated in meth and smeared with the body odour of bad boy ex-boyfriends makes it addictive. There are a couple of dildos inside of it, too, knocking around and causing havoc. It's a hell of a ride to be on.

During a visit to my apartment after work one afternoon, Sonia sat down in the chair opposite me and proceeded to tell me her life story. She was well-dressed, in tight, ass hugging jeans and an imitation leather jacket. She'd straightened her hair with an iron and her lips glistened with gloss. I made her a cup of tea and something to eat. Without knowing it, I'd become her therapist.

As usual, she was flirtatious and covertly sexual, occasionally teasing me by bending over to pick something up, exposing the tip of her thong above the line of her jeans, or leaning forward with her breasts jutting out, stretched tight across her t-shirt: ripe fruit ready to pluck. I could barely contain my lust.

Her story was one I'd heard before from other young women, the usual cliché of a teenage girl getting hooked on drugs and bad boys; only to realise, through the love of Jesus, that she'd lost her way and needed to be saved, eventually giving up the drugs but not necessarily the bad boys. She went to church weekly, worked a normal job, and had plans of one day attending university.

Her prior drug use was presumably the cause of her being a few fries short of a Happy Meal. She claimed, among other things, that Jesus spoke to her every day, offering her advice and guiding her continually. She attended a Pentecostal church where people regularly spoke in tongues and rolled around on the floor, overcome by the power of the Holy Spirit.

She rarely stayed long when she visited, even on those occasions when I made her dinner. She was forever in a rush, continually distracted by her phone. Like many young women addicted to technology and social media, she had the attention span and patience of a hyperactive toddler.

"You seem a bit unfocussed," I commented one evening, laughing a little to hide my annoyance. She'd been checking her phone every minute instead of the usual two, and I secretly had an urge to grab it from her and smash it on the floor.

"Sorry," she replied disingenuously, tucking her phone in her handbag. "I just wanted to check if he'd messaged. He hasn't. It's been days."

"Who's 'he'?" I inquired. I hoped my jealousy didn't show. Up to this point I'd assumed she was single.

"Just this guy," she smiled playfully. "An older guy."

"Older, eh? How much older?"

"Um...seventeen years. He's forty-two."

Shocked, I almost spat out my tea. I was older than her, true, but not by that much. Damn, he was old enough to be her dad.

"He's a farmer. Used to work as a pastor. I know him from church. Last week he invited me over for coffee, and things got kind of serious."

Long story short, the farmer and former pastor, Bob, ploughed her right there on his living room couch after they'd had their "coffee."

Sonia freely admitted that she was infatuated with Bob. From then on, whenever we got together, she talked about nothing else but him and their relationship. She described him as everything a woman desired in a man: muscley, handsome, confident, worked on cars in his spare time, played it cool and casual. He was, I inferred, the ultimate Chad.

Unfortunately for Bob, he was in the midst of a messy divorce. His wife had left town and moved far away to the city, taking the kids with her. Sonia, whose sympathy for Bob was annoyingly evident, made sure to keep me informed of every excruciating detail of what was going on in the guy's wreck of a life.

It didn't take a genius to realise that Bob, now single and horny, was using Sonia for sex; he had no intention of having a relationship with her. Deep down she sensed this but refused to acknowledge it; she was having too much fun. She spoke freely about their steamy sex life, alluding to the fact that the taboo element of being involved with a much older guy who was still technically married turned her on in a way that no other relationship had before.

Although part of me was tired of hearing about Bob and his dramas, not to mention how good he was in bed, another part of me was amused and fascinated by the topic, in a voyeuristic kind of way. It afforded me a unique and very intimate glimpse into the female psyche.

My overarching goal was to have sex with Sonia. She'd already exhibited a hint of interest in me. I figured that, if I stuck around long enough as a friend, she'd realise what a piece of shit Bob was and choose me instead. Surely it was just a matter of time before their relationship failed. All I needed to do was play my cards right and be patient.

Whenever Sonia was on the outs with Bob, which was often, I'd receive a text message from her to catch up. Either she'd come over to my place for dinner, or, occasionally, we'd go for a drive somewhere.

One Saturday afternoon we took a trip to the beach. During the drive there, the conversation inevitably came around to her relationship with Bob. At one point she took out her phone and showed me several photos of the guy. He looked exactly the way I imagined—blonde, muscley, square-jawed, eyes brimming with confidence.

"Do you think he's hot?" she asked.

"Um, I really wouldn't know," I replied. "I'm a guy."

She was silent a long time as she continued scrolling through the photos. The enormous admiration she felt for her on-again, off-again boyfriend was apparent with each delicate swipe of her finger across the screen. She reminded me of a 1960s teenage girl obsessing over her favourite Beatle. It was sickening to watch.

Later, at the beach, she again brought up the topic of Bob's extraordinary studliness. "I guess I can see why women find him appealing," I admitted.

She nodded, smiling inwardly. "When I first met him, I knew straight away there was something special about him."

"Special how?"

"He was just so...confident. He walked right up to me, and instantly we connected." She paused, thinking, then her expression turned despondent. "He thinks I'm too young. He told me he wants a partner who can help him look after his kids. He's been using dating sites. I'm so sure he's seeing other girls behind my back."

I was tempted to say, 'So, let me get this straight, the guy has no intention of being in a relationship with you, or being exclusive with you, yet you still want to be with him? That's fucking crazy.' Instead, I said, "You deserve better."

She didn't answer. For minutes we walked in silence. Every now and then a pebble or shell would catch her eye and she'd crouch down to pick it up. Suddenly she stopped, turned to look me. "He's not as bad as he sounds. I know he's keeping his options open, but I also know he really cares about me."

I said nothing, merely nodded.

As Sonia and I started spending more time together, I noticed significant fluctuations in her mood, almost as if she were two distinct, contradictory personalities. Some days she was pleasant, almost thoughtful, playing the role of the good Christian girl who wanted to straighten out her life. Other times she acted like a spoilt, ghetto bitch who wanted to rebel against God himself, just to make mummy and daddy angry.

Of course, young women with troubled pasts who speak to Jesus and fuck guys old enough to be their dad can hardly be expected to be psychologically stable. Regardless, her unpredictable fluctuations in personality spun me out; from one day to the next, I had no idea whether she'd present herself as a "good girl" or a "bad girl."

One morning, while possessed by the latter personality, she sent me a text that read, "Guess what I just did?" It was accompanied by a photo she'd taken on her phone of moist bed linen. It emerged that she'd had crazy, dirty sex with Bob, and, feeling horny the next day, had decided to grind up and down on her sheets.

Whereas, before, Sonia had been subtly flirtatious and sexual with me, now she was overtly so. Or was she? What, precisely, was she trying to achieve by telling me about the fact that she'd masturbated all over her sheets? Was she trying to make me jealous and sexually frustrated? Did she want me to man-up and fuck her? She'd been giving me mixed messages for weeks now, leaving me deeply confused.

One evening, following a fight with Bob, she insisted on staying over at my place, bringing with her a bag of clothes and a toothbrush. I suspected it was because she had nowhere else to stay. The thought that it might lead to sex was definitely on my mind, but I wasn't going to get my hopes up. Maybe she just needed some company.

She was happy to share my bed on the condition

that we remain fully clothed. Once under the covers, however, she became irritable and defensive. Then began the litany of complaints: my mattress was not soft enough, the linen not fresh enough, and she felt cramped and uncomfortable.

Most of all, she was put off by the beads of condensation on the ceiling. This was the middle of winter, and my place had a tendency to get damp during the colder months, even with the heater running at its maximum setting. Occasionally the droplets would come loose and splash me in the face as I lay in bed. The only solution was to remove them using a mop.

I quickly located the mop and got to work. I'd managed to remove most of the droplets when, all of a sudden, she thrust herself out of bed, grabbed her bag and told me she wanted to leave. It was at that point I learned a valuable lesson: living in a cold, shitty apartment with condensation on the ceiling is hardly a way to charm the ladies.

Grabbing my coat from the rack, I told her I'd walk her to her car. It was dark out and bitterly cold. As we crossed the two blocks to her vehicle, several times I begged her to reconsider, suggesting that, if she wanted, I could move the bed into the other room, where there was less condensation on the ceiling. My pleas were dismissed with an irritated shrug, further compounding her bad mood.

The feeling of rejection that accompanies the realisation that you've blown your chance with a woman, that there's nothing you can do to make her sleep with you, that she thinks you're pathetic and needy and have no value, is like being punched in the balls and the guts simultaneously. And yet I remained convinced that I'd win her over eventually, simply by being a nice guy.

"Let me give you a hug," I offered, with arms outstretched.

I hugged her lightly, platonically. As I pulled away, her eyes lit up with anger. "If you try anything, I'll smash your fucking face in."

She climbed into her Suzuki and sped off. I gave a feeble wave and plodded home, utterly depressed at the outcome of the evening and puzzled by Sonia's hostile reaction to my hugging her. Was it possible she'd been sexually abused in the past? Or was her response simply one of extreme repulsion?

I headed straight to bed but my mind remained unsettled, gloomy. I lay awake in the dark for hours, squeezing the pillow for comfort. How, I wondered, did my life end up like this? Plenty of guys managed to get laid, including guys with little to offer, so why not me? Why had the gods singled me out for celibacy?

As Sonia's relationship with Bob began to disintegrate, I started receiving texts from her on a more frequent basis. No longer were her messages friendly and chatty but desperate and occasionally rude. She was in full ghetto mode at this point. The good Christian girl had vanished.

"Can I borrow $30? for ciggys?" she messaged one evening after work. When I texted back, "Sorry, but I don't lend people money unless they really need it," she became angry, texting back, "Screw you, then." This was followed by an apology of sorts, in which she explained she was going through a stressful time

She had good reason to be stressed. Her obsession with Bob was causing her life to spiral out of control. So as to spend more time with Bob, she'd relocated from her parent's house to a rental property situated in the same town as where he resided—this despite his not wanting her around, except, of course, for sex. Though it meant he was now just a stone's throw away, it also meant spending two exhausting hours on the road each day just to get to work and back. It was insane, the kind of thing a stalker would do.

About a week after texting me begging for money, she sent me a short message in which she informed me that she was unwell and taking antiviral medication. It was flu season, so I figured she'd caught the flu and was experiencing complications. I was wrong. She didn't have the flu. She had herpes.

I wasn't surprised she'd contracted herpes from Bob. It was apparent to Sonia at this point in their relationship that Bob fucked around a lot, earning him a reputation around town as someone incapable of keeping his dick in his pants. She further revealed that his favourite position was anal, and that he preferred to "raw dog" it rather than use a condom. This she allowed, knowing that if she didn't make him happy, he'd show her the door. To not please Bob was out of the question. Anything for the dominant alpha.

I was both fascinated and disgusted by Sonia's relationship with Bob. Disgusted for obvious reasons, and fascinated because it afforded me a revealing glimpse into the dark side of the female psyche. She liked to share, too, and would tell me the most intimate details about their sex life. How, for example, Bob liked it rough, throwing her around the bed like a ragdoll, sometimes whipping her on the ass with his belt; and how he demanded to be addressed as "daddy" and "sir," lest he whip her harder.

Bob, clearly, had mastered the art of "treating 'em mean and keeping 'em keen." He treated Sonia like dirt and she loved him for it. The worse he treated her, the stronger her attraction towards him. Even after he'd given her herpes, she still thought he was the most wonderful man in the world. Not just any man, either, but a man of God. A former pastor, no less.

At the time, I was perplexed as to why a girl would be attracted to a guy who treats her like shit. It didn't make the least bit of sense to me. It was uncanny, counterintuitive, paradoxical, like something out of quantum physics. Aren't you supposed to be nice to a girl in order to make her like you and want to sleep with you? Like buy her flowers, show her that you care, express your sensitive side, and take her out on romantic dates?

Still, I remained convinced that being nice to Sonia was an effective long-term strategy. I believed, as simps do, that it's the nice guy who finally wins the girl, provided he's persistent and patient enough. According to this view, once she's had enough of being mistreated by the bad boy and it dawns on her that the nice guy has loved and supported her all along, she'll fall into the arms of the nice guy. That's how it plays out in the movies; therefore, it must be true.

I was still hopeful that, in time, Sonia would sleep with me. Though I was hardly pleased she'd contracted herpes, an infection both incurable and highly contagious, I figured a condom would fix the problem, if and when we took that step. In the meantime, we were hanging out as friends and she was continuing to share with me intimate details about her sex life. The latter satisfied my voyeuristic tendencies. Later I'd reflect on the strange dynamic of our relationship and come to realise that I wasn't just a simp but to some degree a cuck as well.

One Saturday, a couple of weeks later, I received a message from Sonia inviting me over to her new house. Since taking the antiviral medication, she said, the worst of her herpes symptoms had abated. Yet, while her physical condition had improved, her emotional state was worse than ever. Bob had met someone else and dumped her, leaving her heartbroken, lonely and in need of a friend. I couldn't have been happier with the news.

"I'd like to visit," I replied, "but it's a long drive to your place, so give me twenty minutes to think about it."

My response was purposely misleading. I'd already decided I was going to visit, only I wanted to leave her hanging slightly to create a sense of anticipation. My approach from now on was to play it cool, much the way Bob had done, by not acting too eager or making myself too available. I'd blown my last couple of chances with Sonia. I wasn't going to let that happen again.

I started getting undressed in preparation to shower when I heard my phone buzz with her reply: "I know it's a long drive, but I really need someone to talk to. You can always stay over. Pretty please?" I kept my response short and devoid of enthusiasm: "Okay. Be there in a couple of hours."

I dressed casually, in a pair of jeans and a red and white flannelette shirt. Before hitting the road, I made sure to pack deodorant and a fresh change of clothes. On the way, I stopped off at a supermarket to purchase a pack of condoms. The last thing I wanted was to catch herpes.

The town where she lived was a hellhole, its only notable attraction being a brown, swampy river, filled with discarded chip packets and *Coke* bottles, that zigzagged through the heart of the town. I was hit with feelings of dread and hopelessness the moment I passed the "Welcome To" sign.

With a population of around 4,000, most of them hillbillies, troubled youths, and impoverished elderly pensioners, it was hardly a hive of activity and culture.

Its sole major employer, an abattoir, had shut its gates about a decade ago, and it had since gained a reputation for backyard methamphetamine production. Here was a place where dreams came to die, where the forces of decay and suffering reigned supreme, where the only way out was at the end of a bottle or by means of a needle and bent spoon.

Driving down the main street, it felt like a ghost town. The only businesses open, as far as I could tell, were a bottle shop and, at the other end of the main street, a general store stocked with little else but canned food, soft drink and lollies. Every other place was either shut for the day or entirely vacant.

Sonia's house was surprisingly agreeable, if not a little on the bland side. She made me a cup of herbal tea and we sat down together on the couch in the living room, within a precious patch of warmth from the slanted afternoon sun.

I didn't need to ask her how she was doing; her appearance told me everything. Her eyes were red from having cried recently. Over Bob, of course. She'd dressed lazily, in a faded grey t-shirt and a pair of highly revealing yoga pants. I could feel the tightness in my underwear growing.

"I'm going to have a nap," she said listlessly. "Feel free to watch TV." Without uttering another word, she stretched out like a cat and lay down beside me, eyes closed, her ass poking out in my direction.

Luckily, I'd brought along my copy of *The Catcher in the Rye*. Over the next hour or so, I tried to read. But the tightness in my pants was distracting, and every now and then I couldn't help but steal a glance at Sonia's perfect ass. She mustn't have been completely asleep, because occasionally she'd wiggle it provocatively. If her objective was to drive me insane with lust, it was working.

When afternoon came, we decided to go for a leisurely drive, finally ending up in a nearby, seaside town. Already it was early evening and we were both hungry. Sonia pointed across the road to a quaint, red-brick hotel with a sign out the front offering "counter meals" and suggested we have dinner there.

Once inside, I stood warming myself in front of the open fireplace in the dining area while I waited for Sonia to visit the toilet. She'd given me her handbag to mind. This I was proud to do—it made me feel needed, useful, like a boyfriend. We found a table at the back, away from the rabble at the bar. Sonia was, as always, broke, so I offered to pay for the meals and drinks.

Gradually her mood began to brighten, her face adopting an impish smirk. It was hard to maintain a conversation with her, lost as she was in her own little world. She kept taking photos of the two of us and posting them on *Facebook*, then going back to the bar for another vodka and orange. I was confused—she'd never taken photos of the two of us before. Only later did I learn that the *Facebook* posts were directed at Bob, for the purpose of trying to make him jealous. I was the sucker in the middle, a prop used to manipulate a guy who no longer had feelings for her, if indeed he had any to begin with.

I made sure we left the hotel before either of us became too drunk, and while I still had money in my bank account. Of the two of us, I was the less intoxicated, so I took the wheel. Sonia sat in the passenger seat, silent and brooding, her bad mood from earlier having suddenly reappeared. I knew better than to ask her how she was feeling; I didn't want to hear her talk about Bob again. To hell with that guy. He'd lost, I'd won. Very soon Sonia would be mine.

It had grown dark outside. Wispy grey clouds streaked past a gibbous moon. The ocean in the distance shimmered, ominous and strangely sentient. Part way through the drive, Sonia put on some Taylor Swift, turning the volume up so loud it caused my eardrums to ache. I didn't dare object to the volume of the music. She was in a troubled mood and the vehicle belonged to her; it wasn't my place to say anything.

Twenty minutes later, she told me to pull over on the side of the road to allow us to switch positions. This accomplished, we continued on our way. My manner of driving, she remarked, was "awkward," and consequently she didn't feel comfortable with me at the wheel. She told me about a guy she'd once dated whose clumsy driving put her off so much that she lost all attraction for him and ended up not fucking him. There goes my chance, I thought.

We soon arrived back at her place. My staying the night was assumed on account of the late hour. I had objections about climbing into bed with her, but did so anyway, removing all of my clothes except my t-shirt and underwear. I still wanted to get laid. I'd come this far. To bail now would be cowardly.

As we lay beside each other in the dark, she remained glued to her phone. The glow of the screen reflected off her face, lending her features a strange, almost demonic aspect. It was evident that Bob hadn't reacted to her *Facebook* posts, because her mood remained one of bitchiness and silence.

Five minutes later she put her phone down. It was then that I made my move, engaging her in a conversation about sex. Very soon we were fondling each other and making out; and soon after that she let me pull down her underwear and touch her below.

The events that followed I've already described. She

told me I "wasn't doing it right" and that she wanted me to leave, so I ended up driving home in the early hours of the morning. The following day she sent me a text explaining that she no longer wanted to be friends. After that I never heard from her again.

Several years later, I bumped into her at the supermarket. I was in the middle of bagging my groceries when I heard a voice beside me say, "Hi, Chuck." I spun around and there she was, standing at the adjacent self-serve checkout. Little about her had changed. She had the same crazy eyes, wore the same mischievous expression, and deep inside her there lurked, as before, the same potential to ruin a man's life.

"Hi," I mumbled. "How's it going?"

"Blessed, as always. God has a mission for me."

"Really? What's that?"

"Next year I'm studying to become a social worker. It's my calling."

"Congratulations. I'm pleased to hear it."

She took a step closer so no one could hear. Suddenly her expression darkened. "You know, Chuck, I'm so glad we stopped being friends."

"Um, okay." I was speechless but intrigued all the same.

"I needed a friend and you used me. I now have a guy in my life who treats me right."

"So you're back together with Bob, then?"

"No! Someone else. You know, I don't even know why you're speaking to me right now. I told you to leave me alone."

I was tempted to point out the absurdity of her statement, but, before I had a chance to do so, she'd stormed off in a huff. I took one last, sneaky glance at her amazing ass.

There's a part of us that's in touch with the stark, objective truth of any given situation. This part of us, if we're prepared to listen to what it has to say, can guide us in recognising when we've fucked up and how. Some call it our "gut instinct." Others use more spiritual terms like "higher self," "the God within" and "Buddha nature."

I prefer the term "conscience," because it's really our sense of right and wrong and its purpose is to help us correct our behaviour and make better decisions.

My conscience I've personified. He's a bearded old man who lives in a cabin in the woods. He's occasionally surly, at times an asshole, but ultimately his heart's in the right place and he knows what's best for me. Though he's seen some shit, experienced the absolute lowest of the low, he's neither bitter nor resentful towards humanity or the world.

Today I've come to see him in the hope he can offer me some guidance in becoming less of a simp. Already the conversation is making me uncomfortable and I'm beginning to have second thoughts about making the trip.

"I regret how things worked out between me and Sonia," I say.

The old man scowls. "What's there to regret?! She was a skank with serious daddy issues and a history of drug addiction who used religion as a psychological crutch. She was nuts. Not to mention a serious liability. Were you out of your fucking mind?"

"Probably a little," I admit, casting my gaze downward in shame. "I guess I just wanted to sleep with her. She had an amazing ass. I was so close, too!"

He sighs. "Amazing ass or not, she was crazy. Never forget the number one rule: don't stick your dick in crazy. Besides, she didn't want to fuck you. Not really. Women fuck guys they have genuine desire for, not because they find them nice. Desire is not something you can negotiate over tea and biscuits. Either a woman wants to fuck you or she doesn't."

"Really? If she didn't want to sleep with me, then how do you explain the incident where things got hot and heavy?"

"Ha! She needed a story to make her ex-boyfriend jealous. Sex—*actual sex*—was never part of the plan. She had you locked in the friendzone and she'd thrown away the key. Once you're in the friendzone, you can say goodbye to getting your dick wet. You'd have to be a fucking Harry Houdini to escape that one."

"But why keep me around at all if she didn't want to have sex with me?"

"For company, attention, entertainment. Because she wanted to feel desired. Because you were weak and easy to manipulate."

"I feel used," I say, indignant. "The whole time she was dangling a carrot in front of my face and I was stupid enough to fall for it!"

"I'd go easy with the self-pity, son. She used you, sure, but only because you allowed it to happen. You practically gave her permission to lead you around by the dick. That's on you, not her. Your sense of self-worth is so lacking that you believe, deep down, that you deserve to be used and mistreated by women. The possibility that you could be loved and respected by a woman, simply for being yourself, is incongruent with the poverty mindset you hold."

2

THE CURSE
OF THE COOMER

I wasn't always a simp. At some point during the course of my development I adopted a simp mentality and this became my reality. Partly I blame pornography for stunting and distorting my sexual growth, for making me a slave and an addict to the booty when I should've been doing better things with my time.

To clarify, I grew up at a time when smartphones still belonged to the realm of science fiction and personal computers and the internet hadn't yet taken over the world. The porno mag was how we got our porn fix. VHS porn existed, too, but those babies were precious and hard to obtain. Only once I'd reached my late-teens to early-twenties did internet porn take off—and that was mainly in the form of pictures, not videos.

Not that we had a computer or the internet. My brother and I grew up skint, the sons of an alcoholic musician and writer who'd long ago surrendered to welfare dependence and a victim mindset; and a hippy, feminist mother who abandoned us when I was four and my brother five. We lived as hillbillies, in a shed unconnected to mains electricity or other basic amenities. Going to the toilet consisted of digging a hole in the ground and squatting over it. Baths we took in an old cast iron tub out the back with a fire underneath.

It was a rough existence, devoid of comfort and parental love, but my brother and I battled on. We were unable to rely on our father, so we learned to rely on ourselves. Every school day we rose early and walked to the end of our driveway to catch the bus. It was on one such morning that I saw my first porno mag. I must've been around 12 at the time. I remember it being cold, windy and overcast. But, then, it was like that most days.

The porno mag, when I spotted it, lifted my mood. It sat there on the shoulder of the highway, partly hidden in the grass, surrounded by plastic bottles and other trash. It was heavily weathered, its pages faded and torn. I approached hesitantly, bent down to take a closer look, all too aware of the forbidden nature of the item and the risk of getting caught.

I spent a moment poking and prodding it with a twig, as if I were inspecting the remains of a dead but very exotic animal. Still using the twig, I lifted the front cover. I was instantly rewarded with a glorious sight: a blonde with huge tits, the nipples pink and fiercely erect. It was the most spectacular thing I'd ever seen.

The image both scared and thrilled me. A pulse of electricity passed through my 12-year-old body, a sensation both pleasant and strangely unsettling. For a moment, the porno mag and I became one. I wasn't just looking at those glorious big tits, I was exploring their peaks and valleys, nestled between the cleavage, lost in a tit savanna. The trance ceased when from behind me

I heard my brother shout, "The bus is coming!"

At the age of sixteen, I was sent to live with my mother in rural Victoria, at a Buddhist retreat centre where she worked as a caretaker, while my brother remained living with our father. I hated my new environment, resented my mother, so tried to escape the only way I knew how: by going inward.

Over time, I became a kind of horny vampire, holed up all day in my bedroom, shunning sunlight and social interaction, frustrated and angry with the world and myself. Listening to angst-ridden pop music and fantasising about girls were about the only activities I engaged in, besides masturbation, of course, which I practised religiously at least three times a day. My mother didn't know what to do with me. I don't blame her either.

One school holiday, desperate to have a break from me, she bought me a bus ticket to Sydney. I was to stay with my sister for two weeks, at the share-house she occupied in the bohemian suburb of Newtown.

My sister was a wild, sexually promiscuous woman, fond of getting high and visiting alternative nightclubs. Short, chesty and blonde, she attracted men easily, but occasionally slept with women as well, if only for the sake of variety and excitement. Her relationships were turbulent and short-lived. She had a tendency to burn through partners at an astonishing rate; I could barely keep up with who she was dating.

During the day she worked as a mistress at an S&M brothel, nailing men's scrotums to planks, delivering golden showers, whipping slaves in gimp-suits, and performing other kinky acts for the benefit of wealthy perverts. The stories she'd tell of her escapades at work were a source of continual entertainment—gritty, disturbing, visceral, but also full of humour. She enjoyed being a mistress. Mainly, though, she did it for the money; for a young woman who'd dropped out of high school and had no qualifications, it paid extremely well.

My sister lived with two other weirdos: her boyfriend, Dan, who worked in retail selling computers, and her friend and occasional lover, Carly. Carly was tall and sexy, with dark, straight hair and large bosoms. As a horny sixteen-year-old, I could barely glance in her direction without cracking a boner.

She reminded me of an Amazonian warrior woman—tough, fearless, proud, and capable of eating men for breakfast. Like most teenage boys, I was partial to the fantasy of being seduced and dominated by an attractive older woman; and I hoped that the seductress in question, the one who'd ravage my helpless, young flesh, would be Carly. I'm sure this later fed into my obsession with MILF and cougar porn.

My sister, Carly and Dan all worked full-time, so most days I had the house to myself. I seldom ventured out, except to buy *Mars* bars and cans of *Coke* from the general store down the road. As someone who'd been raised in the country, the hubbub of the city I found overwhelming, to say nothing of my teenage tendency towards introversion and brooding.

Not that I minded being indoors. Like Kevin McAllister in *Home Alone*, the house I treated as my own private wonderland. For eight hours each day, there were no rules or adult supervision. I was free to do whatever I wanted, like drive my remote-control monster truck around the bedrooms and hallways, consume bowl after bowl of cocoa pops, and play video games to the point of severe eye strain.

One day, inspired by boredom, mischief, and the desire to bust a nut, I decided to explore the spare room used for storage at the far end of the house. I was hopeful I'd find some porn, either belonging to my sister or Dan. Working efficiently, I pulled a couple of boxes down and started going through them. It was mostly junk—receipts, old photos, CDs, nothing of value or interest to me. Still I persisted, digging through box after box of junk.

It was in the fifth or sixth box that I finally hit the mother load: a stack of about fifty *Penthouse* magazines in mint condition, which I could only assume belonged to Dan. Short of actually getting laid, preferably by Carly, this was the boner equivalent of winning the lottery. It was a randy, teenage boy's dream come true.

From then on until the end of my stay, I spent the majority of my alone time salivating and cracking boners over *Penthouse* babes, periodically visiting the toilet to jerk off. My three favourited pornos I ended up slipping into my suitcase, eventually taking them home with me. Knowing I'd stolen them from Dan troubled my conscience to a degree, but I convinced myself that Dan, assuming he discovered the magazines were gone, wouldn't miss them. Besides, when you're sixteen years old and fiercely horny, your dick takes precedence over morality every time.

I treasured those pornos, kept them for years. My favourite was a special edition featuring a blonde MILF performing various erotic poses at home while going about her daily housework: lying spread-eagle on the couch while holding the vacuum cleaner nozzle to her snatch, getting flour all over her tits while baking a cake, and so on. It was delightfully filthy stuff, but also rather tame by today's standards. There was no insertion of giant dildos up mangled and overly-stretched orifices, and, best of all, no alpha dude dominating the scene with his giant pork sword. It was just the woman on her own, flashing her pussy exclusively for my enjoyment.

I found other porn in the spare room besides those copies of *Penthouse*. Weird, kinky stuff that left me feeling deeply confused. The strangest item was a booklet, amateurishly produced, featuring images of men in nappies, some of them locked in cages, being simultaneously cared for and punished by highly dominant nursemaids. One of the men, having pissed his nappy, was getting it changed by one of the nurse-maids, a heavily tattooed woman with enormous tits and pierced nipples. He'd been a very naughty boy, according to the caption. Clearly Dan had some unorth-odox tastes. No wonder he'd chosen to date my sister.

During my stay, I heard sexual activity almost nightly, most of it between Carly and the various dudes she brought over for one-night stands, this despite her having a steady boyfriend at the time, a soft-spoken, sensitive guy who adored her (but who clearly had no idea she was cheating on him). One night she came home accompanied by a goth dude, a muscley, long-haired animal covered in piercings and tattoos, who she then proceeded to fuck loudly in the room adjacent to mine.

I wasn't so much turned on as I was disturbed by their loud, satanic fucking. It went on for hours. I heard everything—moans, grunts, whipping sounds, cries of pain. At one point the goth dude stumbled out of the room dressed in nothing but a pair of boxer-shorts, bleary-eyed and high, a huge, dopey grin plastered across his face, to ask me if I could help him with a light, before stumbling back into the room for round two.

Carly liked to boast about the rapidly accumulating notches on her bedpost, no doubt because of the atten-tion it garnered her. The next morning, as we sat eating breakfast, she jokingly apologised for keeping me up. Embarrassed, I lied and said I hadn't heard anything. With a mischievous glint in her eye, she launched into a long and detailed account of the events of the night before.

She'd first met the goth dude at a club, she said. After fucking him at Camperdown Cemetery behind a tombstone, she'd then brought him home to fuck him some more. He had a huge dick, which meant she'd had to lube up her pussy more than once. They'd used hot wax and whips on each other.

All of this had taken place behind her boyfriend's back, but of course she failed to include that part.

Up till then I'd been under the illusion that women weren't as sexual as men; that, unlike men, they didn't fuck for the sake of fucking. Clearly, I'd been wrong. Not only was it okay for a woman to be sexually promiscuous, even at the expense of her boyfriend, it was celebrated as a form of female empowerment.

My sister, a self-proclaimed feminist, echoed this same sentiment when she told me that for millennia women had been brutally oppressed by men, prevented from expressing their deepest sexual desires. Now, for the first time in history, they were free to explore their sexuality, to fuck whomever they wanted, however they wanted, without being unfairly judged by society.

Of course, I wasn't yet old enough to have a mature opinion on these issues. I knew virtually nothing about the world, about life, about women. I was a virgin. I hadn't even kissed a girl. I simply assumed that my sister, being older and smarter than myself, knew what she was talking about. I didn't dare question her "wisdom."

All I cared about at the time was keeping my precious porno mags hidden and not getting caught jerking off. I kept them tucked away in the bottom of my suitcase on the bus trip back to my mum's place. At home, I found the perfect hiding place for them: under my mattress.

Later, while living once again with my dad, I decided to burn them. I had a love-hate relationship with my porno mags: I loved jerking off to the naked babes but hated myself for doing so. I also hated having to hide them. The shame, guilt and stress of keeping a secret stash of porn in my bedroom was eating away at me. It was a burden I could no longer bear. I would erase the evidence once and for all.

I chose the perfect time to complete my mission: early one morning before school, while both my brother and dad were still asleep. With the porno mags concealed under my shirt, I tiptoed outside to the incinerator, discreetly slipped the mags inside, poured some kerosene over them, and set fire to the dirty fuckers with a match. Instantly the flames leapt upward, tits and ass transformed to ash and thick, black smoke. It was satisfying and cleansing to watch. Sad, too. They'd served me well, those mags, providing me with many joyful moments. I'd miss them like old friends.

That afternoon, upon arriving home from school, I immediately went out to the incinerator to inspect the ashes of my once beloved porno mags. The sight made me go white in the face and nearly piss my pants—they hadn't burnt completely! Patches of magazine remained largely unaffected, still showing pussy, ass, thighs, and nipples. In my haste to destroyed them, I'd forgotten that glossy paper doesn't burn easily. The flames, instead of consuming the magazines, had reduced them to porn confetti.

There was a small garden spade and bucket nearby that we used to empty the incinerator. Frantically, I began scooping the porn confetti into the bucket, making sure to remove every last trace of evidence. Once full, I hauled the now heavy bucket to the large, open pit at the rear of our house. Here I disposed of the contents, throwing on a load of dirt for good measure. It was a sweltering day, and the hasty effort of removing the porn confetti left me exhausted and damp with sweat. I was relieved, however, that I'd pulled it off without a single soul being the wiser.

It turned out I wasn't out of the woods just yet. About a week later, while riding my bike around the property, I spotted something poking out of the grass: a small, glossy piece of paper with singed edges. I dismounted, heart racing, dashed over to pick it up. My fears were confirmed: it was a piece of porn confetti!

It featured a pair of tits, heavily scorched but otherwise discernible to the trained eye. It was clear what had happened: a feral cat or other animal, possibly while looking for food, had scattered the soil that held down the porn confetti, setting it loose on the breeze. For the next hour, I scouted around the yard looking for porn confetti. I ended up with a handful of it.

One afternoon a few days later, I was standing at the kitchen sink washing the dishes when my brother entered laughing like a maniac. "Look what I found," he announced, holding before me a piece of porn confetti. It showed a section of upper thigh and the smallest trace of vagina.

In an effort to conceal my shock and embarrassment, I gave a casual shrug then proceeded with the dishes. "Must've drifted over from the neighbour's yard," I said.

"Probably," he agreed, emitting a final laugh before tossing it in the bin.

There's no thought more likely to make a young man paranoid than that his parents will eventually stumble upon his porno collection and realise what a dirty little pervert he is. It's enough to keep him up at night, tossing and turning in bed, praying to God—or the devil—for a solution or a way out.

Often the pressure of keeping his porno concealed becomes so great that he finally cracks, prompting him to destroy the evidence, as I did. Some young men, on the other hand, are made of sterner stuff, refusing to part with their precious smut no matter what. I knew a guy in high school who constructed a secret compartment in his bedroom wall for the exclusive purpose of stashing his prized collection of *Hustler*.

Porn, as with human remains, is notoriously difficult to destroy, requiring similar methods of disposal. As fans of true crime will know, there are at least several effective ways to dispose of a body: burn it; bury it; or dump it in a lake or at sea. So too with porn. I of course prefer the first method, but that is clearly not always effective.

Two friends of mine, one a similar age to myself, the other a much older man and former Australian senator, both resorted to the third method. The former stuffed his collection of porno mags into a bag, added some rocks for weight, made sure the bag was well-sealed, and hurled the bag into a dam, where it quickly sunk and disappeared. The latter did much the same thing, but with 90s VHS porn.

There are other creative methods of porn disposal. An acquaintance in high school told me how, fearing his mum would find the forbidden item and needing to act quickly, he tore up an entire copy of *Swank* into tiny strips and flushed the strips down the toilet in handfuls. Multiple flushes were required. His mum assumed he had a bad case of the runs.

Porn makes you think of women not as actual people but rather as objects to be won over or worshipped. I suspect it's in part owing to the influence of porn that, as a teenager, I found myself harbouring crushes on girls with whom I stood little to no chance of forming a relationship—either because the attraction wasn't mutual or because we had nothing in common, or both.

I'd spend months, even years, obsessing over one particular girl. I'd daydream about her continually, imagining an entire relationship with her in my head, complete with romantic and intimate milestones like our first kiss. Soul-crushing anxiety, combined with an overly active imagination, would prevent me from ever actually speaking to her.

As a teenager, having a crush on a girl is thrilling and addictive, like a drug. You see her walking by with her friends. You glance briefly in her direction, hoping to catch her eye. She completely ignores you, so you wait till the next time you see her and try again. The lingering possibility, however remote, that she'll eventually reciprocate your interest is enough to motivate you to keep going. All the while, you live small, do nothing bold.

My first major crush was on a girl named Simone. She was dark-haired, introverted, enjoyed horse riding. Her eyes sparkled when she spoke to her friends. I thought she was the most beautiful, delicate creature in the world, like one of Tolkien's elves. When I moved away to another state, I sent her a love letter, addressed to her via the school office. I poured out my heart, confessed how much I liked her, and would she please write me back? She never did. I doubt she even read it. Most likely she tossed it in the bin out of embarrassment.

My next major crush was on a girl named Lisa. Her parents and my mother were acquaintances, both members of the same Buddhist community. She was sixteen; I was nineteen. She had thick, caramel hair that cascaded past her shoulders, luminous blue eyes, and she carried herself with the confidence and poise of a goddess. I was drawn to her femininity with the longing of a thirsty hiker in pursuit of a cool mountain stream on a hot day. She was, in my mind, divine—too perfect to have impure thoughts about. Yet to say that I didn't notice her ample bosoms and pear-shaped physique would be a lie.

I first met her at a Tibetan Buddhist celebration to mark the New Year. Held outdoors under the starry sky, it featured a country band and enough food and alcohol to keep everyone partying for a week. All of the adults, including my mother and her parents, were drunk out of their minds and had no idea—nor cared— what their kids were up to. A teenager can get away with a lot at such an event. Though nervous as hell, I used the opportunity to strike up a conversation with Lisa.

There were several other teenagers present, including Lisa's red-haired younger sister. Considering ourselves too cool to associate with the adults, about five or six of us huddled together in a storage shed out the back, where we spent the next several hours making fun of our parents and their cringeworthy dancing. To my surprise, Lisa laughed at my jokes. Before she left, I asked her for her home phone number and she gave it to me. I told her I'd give her a call sometime.

Call her I did, almost two times a week. This proved problematic. First, I was a poor conversationalist on the phone—awkward, nervous, unnatural, self-conscious. Gone was my ability to charm her or make her laugh, as happens when obsession and the desire to impress replaces casual charm and magical spontaneity. Second, her father, a tall, red-haired gorilla of a man of Dutch and Italian heritage, often the one who answered the phone when I called, made it clear he didn't approve of my contacting his daughter. Fiercely protective of his little girl, though not bold enough to tell me to fuck off, he'd grunt with disapproval, say she was busy, and would I mind calling back, say, next week?

Yet I persisted. I was convinced I'd win her over, not by being sleazy and putting the moves on her like all those other guys, but by being perfectly charming and pure. I'd win her over, I figured, by demonstrating that I valued her first and foremost as a friend. My thinking process could be summed up as follows: *Only bad, sleazy guys want to date girls to have sex with them. I'm not like those bad, sleazy guys. I'm different, unique. I have depth and sophistication. Once she recognises this, she'll fall in love with me.*

No longer comfortable talking to her on the phone, in part because of her dad, I switched tactics: I started sending her amusing emails, demonstrating what a clever and witty writer I was. To my delight, she replied on a consistent basis, complimenting my writing and sharing jokes of her own. Her sense of humour, at least via email, was as left-field as mine. Eventually she suggested that we catch up on the weekend.

She invited me to her house a few weeks later. She lived far away, in the affluent, inner city suburb of Kew; and since I was still too young to drive, I had no other choice but to make the journey via public transport. It took me two gruelling hours but I didn't mind—I would happily have travelled three times that distance to see her. And, besides, girls adore guys who bend over backwards for them, right?

Upon arriving at her house, my anxiety immediately kicked into overdrive. There on the front lawn stood her old man, polishing the white Toyota ute that he used for his job in construction. Dressed in a wifebeater and a pair of shorts, he had a chamois in one hand and a bottle of Turtle Wax in the other. I said hello but he didn't answer, merely nodded, manipulating the chamois in wide, angry circles.

The family home was impressive—a stately, two-storey palace of a place with enough bedrooms to accommodate two families. Once inside, I was invited to eat lunch with Lisa and her parents. Her mum, a suburban housewife with a posh accent, made an effort to engage me in conversation. Her dad remained surly and uncommunicative, eating his chicken sandwich with the seriousness of a mafia boss, his eyes boring uncomfortably into mine.

Afterward, to my intense relief, Lisa suggested we go for a walk around the block. Finally, we had a chance to talk without her parents monitoring our every word and action. As we started down the tree-lined path carpeted with autumn leaves, I finally broke the silence with a question: "So, do you like school?"

She looked at me as if I were a moron. "Yeah, I guess it's okay. What about you?"

"Not really," I answered. "Last week I got dacked in the corridor. It's a rough place."

To be "dacked" is to have your pants pulled down suddenly by another kid, usually from behind, while you're least expecting it.

"That does sound rough," she agreed.

When you're a teenage guy who feels deeply inadequate around girls, having little to offer in the way of looks, popularity, and athletic prowess, there's a tendency to go for the self-deprecation angle: playing the role of the guy who is sensitive, quirky, endearing, and "real," like the nerdy Jewish protagonist in a romantic comedy film, whom the girl eventually chooses over the insensitive jock. This was the angle I was going for with Lisa. I'd watched enough Woody Allen movies to know how to play the part.

"The guys are always playing tricks on me at school," I laughed. "One time, as a joke, they poured a bottle of *Coke* into my locker. Everything got drenched. It was a nightmare cleaning it up."

She nodded but said nothing. The expression on her face said it all—she'd completely tuned out. I no longer existed in her reality.

When we returned to her house, there was a shiny BMW parked out the front; her grandparents had come to visit for the afternoon. Just when I thought the day couldn't get any worse, here was proof that it could and had.

The family gathering took place in the living room. It was a scones and tea affair, accompanied by polite, superficial chatter. I hovered near the corner of the room tentatively nibbling on a scone, while Lisa, sat adjacent to her grandparents, entertained them with stories about her recent holiday to the Gold Coast and news of her academic achievements at the private girl's school she attended.

Taking advantage of a break in the conversation, I announced that my mother was expecting me home and that I ought to be catching my train. After mumbling goodbye to Lisa and her family, who seemed just as relieved by my departure as I was, I was out the door with the speed of a recently released convict.

Once aboard my train, I found an unoccupied seat at the very rear of the carriage, a perfect place to hide and wallow in self-pity. Partway through the journey, I accidentally made eye contact with a junkie.

"What the fuck are you staring at?" he demanded.

"Nothing," I replied. "Sorry."

"You'd better be fucking sorry," he sneered, flashing stained teeth.

As soon as the train reached its next stop, I leapt out of the carriage, fearful the junkie might be in pursuit. About a dozen passengers disembarked, not one of them the junkie.

This wasn't my stop, yet here I was, all because I'd acted like a fucking pussy. I spent an hour at the station waiting for the next train, seated alone on a filthy, gum-covered bench. By the time I arrived home, it was dark, drizzly and cold.

Even after my disastrous visit to her house, I continued to stay in touch with Lisa, but her emails became shorter, less frequent, less intimate. Eventually she mentioned she'd been dating a guy named Beau. He was slightly older than her, had dropped out of school to become an electrician, and—much to Lisa's dad's chagrin—drove a souped-up Nissan Skyline.

As the years passed, other boyfriends followed. There was the drummer in a rock band; the professional poker player; the law student who, at the age of 20, already owned his own apartment in the city. All successful, handsome, popular jocks. Guys with whom I could never measure up. I lost track of all the guys she dated. Last I heard she was working in advertising, making good money and travelling the world.

During my late teens, while I was busy obsessing over Lisa, there were at least a couple of girls—I realise in retrospect—who showed an interest in me romantically, but whom I ended up ignoring and pushing away. One was a tall goth girl with wavy black hair. The other was a short girl with curly brown hair, named Melanie. Though hardly the belle of the ball, she radiated a purity and dynamism that made her the focus of attention in a room.

She was one of the first people in our grade to get her car license. Drove a small, zippy, red Honda. One afternoon I missed the school bus home, so she offered to drop me off. My house was perched on a hill, accessible via a steep, precarious stretch of road that snaked through the trees, with a sharp drop on one side. Especially when wet, it was a death-trap of a road. Being the callous smart-ass that I was, I jokingly demanded that Melanie drive faster. Wanting to please me, she complied, pushing the accelerator down hard.

There's an image burned into my mind, which I still revisit to this day—though I'm not, generally speaking, a nostalgic person. I'm sitting in the passenger seat of Melanie's car. Her knuckles are white from gripping the steering wheel tightly. We both have grins on our faces, mainly from the thrill of having almost died. There's a pleasant tension between us, an electricity, but I don't understand it at the time, nor will I till many years later.

As I unbuckle my seatbelt in preparation to step out, I glance across at her. She looks pretty in the afternoon sun: delicate, feminine, full of life. There's depth and beauty in the way she holds herself. She's a girl who doesn't put on airs or pretend to be someone she's not.

"Thanks for the lift," I mutter.

She nods, eyes twinkling expectantly. "So, I guess I'll see you at school, then?"

"You will," I reply. I step out of the car, shut the door behind me, and start up the driveway to my house. She honks, but I don't turn back and wave.

At the time I didn't want Melanie. Years later I did. I went through a period where I thought about her constantly, kicking myself over opportunities lost and hating with every fibre of my being the harsh, lonely reality of my current situation.

No, I didn't want Melanie. I only had crushes on girls who paid me little to no attention. Bitchy girls were my favourite. Ice queens with cold eyes and no discernible sense of humour. I wanted Veronica Lodge, not Betty Cooper. I developed a proclivity, most likely as a result of watching kinky porn, for being teased and led on by a woman with whom I would never get the chance to have sex.

Speaking of porn, for me it became an obsession in the years following my graduation from high school. I had given up on pursuing girls, since all of the ones I found attractive were unobtainable; and though I desperately wanted to lose my virginity, I had no idea how this might be achieved. Unable to have actual sex, I came to rely on porn to satisfy my sexual needs. Not that it ever truly satisfies; no counterfeit does.

There was always the prostitute option, of course. I knew guys from high school who'd visited brothels in the city, although the stories they related of their experiences with escorts didn't exactly inspire in me a willingness to do the same. The thought of paying a woman to allow me to fuck her both terrified and disgusted me. Many years later, after my divorce, I'd reconsider visiting a lady of the night. That particular experience would go very badly indeed.

I've heard stories of fathers and sons visiting brothels together, generally because the son had turned eighteen and the father decided it was time he "became a man." I had a friend in high school, named Luke, who at one point accompanied his dad to a brothel. It wasn't to lose his virginity, though—he'd lost that years ago, at the age of fifteen. Rather, it was to celebrate his dad's 50th birthday. What better way to mark the occasion, they decided, than by spending the night together banging some whores, just the two of them, father and son.

Luke's dad, a short, fat, jolly man, reminded me of a character from a wacky 80s comedy film, both in appearance and behaviour. He had a habit of ending his sentences with ripples of effeminate laughter. He cherished his wife and they'd been married for years, but somewhere along the way their sex life had died altogether. Shagging the occasional whore, presumably without his better half's knowledge, was his way of compensating for this lack.

A courier driver by day, he was used to cruising the suburbs and had developed an almost uncanny knack for locating the addresses of his clients. On the night of his birthday, however, while searching for a brothel to visit with his son, his expertise fell short. The two found themselves driving around in circles, unable to locate a quality establishment. At one place they inquired, the women were extremely fat. At another, all of the girls were ugly except one and she was already booked out for the night.

Finally, after another half-hour of driving around, they settled on an establishment where the women weren't exactly hot but attractive enough to facilitate their desire to get off. Luke chose a shy Pilipino woman; his dad, since it was his birthday, decided to treat himself to "the works," opting for a tall, heavy-set black woman, who gave him, he said, "the best fuck of his life."

Luke's dad, incidentally, owned an extensive collection of VHS porn, and whenever I visited, father and son would gleefully load me up with bags of porno tapes. It wasn't the kind of porn that appealed to my tastes; most of it was anal and very low quality. I was grateful, nonetheless, for the free porn. It made my dismal existence a little more tolerable.

My life at this point had taken a downward turn. I'd spent years studying hard in high school, making education the focus of my life, only to achieve less than impressive grades in the final exams. Feeling like a failure, I figured I wasn't cut out for university. What followed was a succession of labouring jobs—vineyard work, demolishing and renovating houses, mowing lawns, and clearing out gutters. As much as I enjoyed some of this work, it paid little more than pocket money and did nothing to put me on a career path.

Time passes quickly when you're adrift and without purpose and a sense of meaning, with little to look forward to but the next porn-induced orgasm. Except Luke, the few friends I'd made in high school had moved away, never to be seen again. Some to attend university. Others because of relationships with girls. Others because, well, life. Gradually I became a loner, isolating myself in my room with the curtains drawn tight, sleeping in till ten in the morning on those days I wasn't required to work.

At that stage I was living at a Buddhist retreat centre in the forest, where my mother worked as a caretaker. Multiple times a year its rooms would fill up with re-treatants, men and women of all ages seeking spiritual enlightenment. The community was led by a Tibetan lama, whom we addressed as Rinpoche.

It was, I realised years later, a cult of sorts. After the Rinpoche died, rumours began to leak out of sexual relations between himself and a number of his female students. Though married, he'd been regularly enlightening his students—only the young, attractive ones, of course—in more ways than one.

I, too, harboured secrets of a sexual nature, though they involved pixelated women, not actual women. Almost every night after my mum had gone to sleep, I'd tiptoe out of my room, laptop under my arm, and make my way down to the office. There I'd remain seated at the desk with the lights switched off, viewing and downloading porn into the early hours of the morning, now and then ducking out with a boner for a masturbation break.

These were the frustrating days of dial-up internet, when you had to wait five minutes for a single JPEG to load. I was dedicated, however, and extremely horny. I was a porn ninja, a true warrior of the one-eyed trouser snake. Still, I wasn't satisfied—I wanted more porn, delivered faster. My appetite had no limits.

One night, as an experiment to see if it would increase the speed of my internet connection, I decided to plug my computer into a different phone line—the one that led into Rinpoche's private residence, where he stayed during retreats. There was no retreat on at the time; Rinpoche was absent. All I had to do was switch one phone line with another. It was simple and it worked—the images loaded faster.

Over the next couple of months, I was in the Buddhist realm of the gods, viewing and downloading porn to my heart's content. I stored as much of it as I could on floppy discs, to be enjoyed the next day in the privacy of my room. I stopped when, one afternoon, I heard my mother say something to a friend about "Rinpoche's extremely high phone bill."

The exact price of the bill I never found out. All I know is that it elicited an investigation of sorts. A technician was called in to inspect the phone lines. Questions were asked, though luckily no suspicion fell on me. My mother was on edge for at least a couple of weeks, looking pale and worried.

As for the karmic consequences of my actions, that's

between me and the Buddha.

"That's quite a story," says the old man.

I can tell he means it not in a condescending way. There's genuine compassion in his voice.

"To paraphrase what you told me, you spent a large portion of your youth doing two things: jerking off to porn and obsessing over girls who weren't interested in you, only to end up lonely, without a girlfriend, and forced to rely on porn as your only sexual outlet. In my estimation, that's tragic."

I feel like a failure, a fuck up. There's a knot of shame in my chest, eating me from the inside out. What the old man said is true, and to acknowledge the truth is sometimes painful. Through gritted teeth I say, "That's more or less what happened, yes."

The old man looks me straight in the eyes. "I'd say it's precisely what happened." After a pause, he adds, "Are you familiar with the Biblical definition of sin?"

"I guess. To murder, rape, steal, lie. To do things that God doesn't approve of."

"It actually has a deeper definition. It means to miss the mark, to fall short of one's God-given potential."

"Interesting," I nod. "Your point?"

"My point is that your story is of someone who sinned. How? Because you lacked the wisdom and courage required to take advantage of the unique opportunities presented to you, thus missing the mark. When we're young, our lives are rich in potential and opportunities are abundant. As we get older, opportunities are fewer and further between. It's a sad fact of existence that some opportunities only come once. A missed opportunity has the potential to set us on a path in life that isn't favourable to our growth and development, as opposed to a path that is. Melanie liked you, for instance, and she would've made a fine girlfriend, only you snubbed her to pursue some classy girl from the suburbs. You chose superficiality over authenticity, and for this you paid a price."

"Gee, thanks," I respond. "I admit I fucked up, okay? But I don't see how that makes me a sinner!"

"It does. Think about it: to sin is to fail to recognise, exploit and nurture those opportunities that God has granted you in accordance with your unique nature."

"You seem to be implying that the notion of sin is tied up with the notion of identity. Correct?"

"Exactly. People sin because they don't know themselves. They're convinced they're somebody or something they're not. They construct entire false identities and attempt to act them out. Lo and behold, it doesn't work! A life lived inauthentically is a life bereft of accomplishment, meaning and satisfaction. It's a hollow kind of existence. The sinner may experience short-term satisfaction. He may even make something of himself in a superficial sense. Long-term, though, he pays the ultimate price: he finds that his hopes, dreams and ambitions have amounted to nothing, resulting in misery and disillusionment. All because he chose to take a short-cut in life rather than put in the effort to better understand himself. Because he missed the mark. Because he chose to live not in reality but fantasy."

"Hence why porn addiction is so common among simps?"

The old man smiles, pleased by my ability to grasp what he's saying. "Absolutely. Pornography is pure fantasy and escapism. So is pretending you're the kind of guy who's an equal and compatible match with a rich, posh girl from the inner suburbs. What were you thinking? Did you have any idea who you were back then?"

"Evidently not," I admit.

"Regardless, you're beginning to understand this very important principle: wherever you find simping you also find fantasy and escapism. You find laziness too."

"Why laziness?"

"Because, again, the simp chooses fantasy over reality. He believes deep down that he isn't cut out for real life. Fantasy is the next best thing. It's a cheap substitute, the lazy way out. Does it not take less effort to whack off to porn than to develop the charisma and social aptitude required to talk a girl into sleeping with you?

"Sure, it does. But I'm not lazy. If anything, I put in too much effort with girls. It's what makes me a simp in the first place."

"Bullshit. You were lazy. And cowardly. You even admitted that you pursued girls who weren't interested in you while ignoring the ones who were. In this way, you set yourself up for rejection. Subconsciously you wanted to fail. Why? Because failing is easy. Once you've failed you can throw in the towel and tell yourself you don't have what it takes. Winning, on the other hand, requires guts, determination, effort and sacrifice."

I shrug. "There's a hole in your argument. You're saying I'm lazy for pursuing girls who aren't interested in me because it guarantees rejection, yes? And subconsciously I want to fail, right?"

The old man nods.

"Then how do you factor in the handful of successes I've had with women? If your logic is correct, I'd still be a virgin."

The old man strokes his beard in contemplation. "I haven't heard your entire story yet, but I'm going to assume that your 'successes,' as you call them, were easy victories. You see, the simp sexual strategy is dual in nature: he either focuses on girls who are so outside of his league that he'll never get to fuck them. Or, again being lazy and cowardly, he goes for the low hanging fruit."

"The low hanging fruit?"

"The whores, sluts, the loose women. They could also be women he isn't particularly attracted to, but who, because they're attracted to him, make the first move."

Finding no reason to disagree, I keep silent.

3

THINKING WITH YOUR DICK & HITTING ROCK, NOT BOTTOM

According to the Asian hooker's instructions, I was to park my car outside the hotel and wait for her text notifying me to enter the building.

So far I'd waited fifteen minutes. Still no text.

The hotel was a pale grey monstrosity that stood precariously on a steep hill. It resembled a lunatic asylum from an 80s horror film—box-like, solidly constructed, isolated from its surroundings, and neglected to the point of disrepair.

I took a deep breath to calm my nerves. Maybe I should get the fuck out of here? Split while I still had a chance?

In the rear-view mirror, I watched a fat, balding, fiftyish man in blue overalls and a grease-stained wife-beater exit the establishment and shuffle across the road to his bomb of a ute. A client? Or a patron who'd come from the direction of the bar?

I hoped it was the latter, not the former. It was one

thing to discover that the Asian hooker plied her trade out of the seediest hotel in town. More disquieting still was the thought that she operated her business like a factory production line, fucking large numbers of clients in quick succession. Not that either precluded the possibility that I'd have a positive experience with the hooker.

I'd come across her ad in the classifieds section of the local paper. Going by the name "Tina," she described herself as "21yo, slim, DD, sweet, and passionate." Allowing for a certain degree of dishonest advertising (I was sceptical of her double-D tits), her attractiveness, I felt, was guaranteed.

Indeed, I'd heard good things about the local Asian hooker scene. All of the girls, apparently, were international students who worked as prostitutes on the side to pay their way through university. Like many guys, I'd come to equate "Asian student" with "sexy."

So far Tina and I had exchanged a few texts for purely logistical purposes. Acting the part of the quintessential Asian whore, she ended each sentence with "baby." For example: "I make sure you have good time, baby." Her unwieldly use of English reminded me of a certain famous scene from the movie *Full Metal Jacket*, though it was not without its ability to arouse.

Suddenly my phone buzzed. It was a message from Tina: "Come to room 22, baby. I'm ready for you."

This was it. To back out at this point would be cowardly. Summoning every ounce of courage I possessed, I hopped out of the car and started up the hill towards the hotel, squinting against the setting sun.

My encounter with Tina would not go smoothly, but of course I didn't know that yet.

Divorce does strange things to a man's psyche. It's an experience I wouldn't wish on my worst enemy. When you've been together with someone so long that your identities have practically merged, only to find yourself in your mid-thirties unloved, unlovable and completely alone, living in some cold, shitty apartment with mould on the ceiling and cracks in the walls, it's enough to force even the most resilient man to contemplate throwing himself off a bridge.

To help numb the pain, you turn to your good friend, alcohol. You spend nights intoxicated out of your brain, lying on the floor of your apartment, weeping uncontrollably. One evening, overcome by feelings of nostalgia, you make the mistake of looking at old wedding photos and listening to the romantic songs you used to dance to together. This leaves you feeling even more miserable.

So, the next day, you delete the photos and the songs from your hard-drive, wipe the fucker clean, and make a promise to yourself that you'll be better, try harder, quit the drinking and the self-loathing and find yourself a new woman. A girlfriend, or, failing that, a fuck buddy. Because that's what people do, right, get over their ex by dating someone new?

No one is more ignorant and naïve than a man in his thirties or older who's recently divorced and trying to navigate the minefield that is the modern dating market. He's like an inmate who's just been released from prison after a decade spent behind bars: everything he thinks he knows about women, dating, and sex is based on a model that no longer accurately reflects the way the world operates.

Times have changed, yet mentally he's stuck in the past. Social norms are not what they were five years ago, let alone ten or fifteen. Woman are less open and trusting towards men, more superficial and conceited. Toxic feminism reigns supreme. The "patriarchy" is evil and men are the enemy, especially heterosexual white guys. He realises, to his shock, that to ask the wrong woman out on a date is to invite trouble, even accusations of sexual harassment.

He, too, has changed, at least in the physical sense. He's fatter, slower, less attractive. His social skills are rusty, his ability to charm a woman, deplorable. Whereas, years ago, when he was dating in his twenties and brimming with confidence and untapped potential, women would pay him attention, now they look down their noses at him.

Eventually the man realises he's been doing it all wrong: guys don't ask women out anymore, not face-to-face in any case. That's what internet dating's for. There's this app called *Tinder*, and it's where all the single women in his area can be found. Best of all, they're not necessarily after anything serious—most of them want sex. If he creates a *Tinder* profile and cleans himself up a bit, maybe starts hitting the gym a few times a week, he, too, can enjoy all that glorious free pussy!

I created a profile not only on *Tinder*, but on another site called *Plenty of Fish*. Perhaps it was a case of beginner's luck because within the first day I'd matched with numerous attractive women. On day three, I was flirting with a young woman named Marie, and she was keen to meet up for a coffee date.

Her photos were jaw-droppingly impressive. She had honey blonde hair, sensual lips, cat-like eyes, and generous bosoms, and the fact that she was of Swedish heritage on her mother's side, even speaking the language, convinced me I'd netted a rare and beautiful bird indeed. This one was a catch, possibly the woman I'd one day marry.

The following morning, before I'd had a chance to arrange the date, I noticed on the app a new message from Marie. "Morning, handsome," it read. "Why don't you come over tonight after work?" Attached was a photo of her wearing a lacy, pink negligee.

I was so excited, so bowled over by my good fortune, that I almost choked on my second cup of coffee. I'd tried internet dating for only three days and already I was scheduled to get laid that night! Later, as I sat at my desk at work, I found myself cracking a boner while imagining sex with Marie. Would she talk to me dirty in Swedish while we did the deed? I hoped so.

After work, I had dinner, showered, and dressed in my best casual clothes. I watched re-runs of *Myth Busters* while I waited for the clock to strike 9. Marie, a single mother and part-time student, had two daughters, aged five and seven; and since the purpose of my visit demanded privacy, it was agreed that we'd wait for her kids to fall asleep first. I respected this rule: I didn't want her kids bursting into the room while I was busy ploughing their mum.

Marie, it turned out, lived in the roughest suburb in town, an area known for its abundance of ice addicts and welfare recipients, where the vast majority of dwellings were ugly, brick boxes that belonged to the public housing sector.

Finding her place in the dark proved challenging; I had to double back a couple of times. Hers was a public house: plain, brick, just like all the others. I parked out the front, knocked on the door, waited. There were kids' toys strewn around the front yard, and, gazing over the fence, I caught sight of a torn and sun-damaged trampoline in the middle of a backyard so overgrown with weeds that it resembled a small jungle.

The moment she opened the door, I knew I'd made a mistake. The disparity between how she looked in the flesh and how she looked in her photos was jarring. I'd been catfished. She was shorter, fatter, older, with saggy breasts and a small ass. Though she wasn't exactly ugly, I was doubtful I'd be able to get an erection when push came to shove, so to speak.

"Come in," she said with a sheepish grin, holding the door open for me.

I followed her into the kitchen, where she motioned me to a chair at the table. I sat down while she busied herself at the bench preparing tea and coffee. Sat across from me was an older woman, a friend of Marie's from class, who punctuated her sentences with peals of tobacco-stained laughter.

Soon Marie sat down too, handing me a cup of coffee in a mug with *Best Fucking Mum* written on it. I sipped my coffee while the two women chatted, barely able to comprehend or keep pace with the rapid stream of their idiosyncratic dialogue.

Occasionally they'd pause and either Marie or her friend would ask me a question. What did I do for work? Where did I live? Did I have kids? Was I divorced, and, if so, for how long had I been divorced? I answered as honestly as possible, reluctant to expose too much but not wanting to come across as shady either.

It felt more like an interrogation than a conversation. It emerged that both Marie and her friend were psychology students. Instantly it dawned on me why the other friend was present: she'd been brought over to assess my character, to determine whether or not I was potentially dangerous.

I must've been given the all clear, because eventually the friend left, and it was just me and Marie.

Very soon her kids, who'd been playing in their room, emerged like a couple of characters out of a Dr. Seuss book, peddling their tricycles around the living room in circles, throwing bouncy balls against the walls, and loudly demanding candy from their mother. Having finally calmed down, the younger of the two girls kept wanting to hug me, starved of fatherly attention.

I asked Marie about the father. He had no contact with his daughters, she said. She described him as a former cage fighter who'd served time in prison, a hyper-masculine, heavily-tattooed brute of a man. About a year ago, she'd been forced to place a restraining order against him after he'd given her more than a few black eyes.

For the next half-hour, I sat on the couch in the living room watching *The Graham Norton Show* while Marie prepared her daughters for bed, reading them bedtimes stories in Swedish. I continued watching TV while she showered. When she emerged from the bathroom, she was dressed in a negligee—not the pink one from the photo, but a cream-coloured one. She looked okay—not exactly sexy, but fuckable. Beggars can't be choosers, I reminded myself.

She led me to her bedroom. A single lava lamp sat beside a queen size bed, illuminating the space with an eerie pink light. She opened the door of her cupboard, revealing her collection of sex toys and accessories: dildos, vibrators, lubricants, handcuffs, and a butt plug with tail attached. She winked, as if to suggest that our evening was about to get very wild indeed.

It didn't. Marie was on edge, peeking out the window every twenty minutes for reasons she did not wish to explain. On the floor on my side of the bed was an exhausted mother cat and her litter of tiny kittens. They squeaked incessantly. The bed was narrow, uncomfortable, and I was worried I'd accidentally roll out and crush them. Furthermore, the younger daughter refused to go to sleep, bursting into the room at unexpected moments and at one point climbing into the middle of the bed for cuddles.

With the daughter finally out of the room and off to bed, Marie and I started making out. Then, all of a sudden, she complained that she was too tired to continue, suggesting that we get some sleep and have sex in the morning instead. This never eventuated. I had to leave early for work, and, besides, Marie was in a bad mood, seemingly resenting my being there.

Upon her request, I ended up spending one more night in her bed. Again, the same thing happened: Marie glancing out the window every twenty minutes, kittens squeaking at all hours of the night, and boisterous children who refused to sleep, followed by no sex.

By this stage I was friends with Marie on social media. She'd ceased responding to my texts, so I had a thorough scroll through her *Facebook* posts to see if any answers could be gleaned. My suspicions were confirmed: she'd updated her profile to "in a relationship." Her boyfriend was a young guy with sandy-coloured hair who worked as an apprentice mechanic. They'd been together two years and were, apparently, madly in love.

Now it all made sense. At the time we met online, Marie had temporarily broken up with her boyfriend. Feeling alone, or perhaps in an attempt to make her boyfriend jealous, she'd invited me over, seemingly for sex. This explained why she'd been nervously peeking out the window—she was concerned her boyfriend might show up at the house at any moment, and, seeing my car parked out the front, lose his shit. Or perhaps she was disappointed that he didn't. Either way, the two got back together, and since Marie no longer needed me around, I was discarded and ignored like the simp that I was.

Altogether I spent approximately a year on various internet dating sites. I became highly proficient at the messaging part, to the extent that I was able to seduce a woman with my words alone within a period of an hour, prompting them, in a few cases, to send me nudes and dirty videos. I secured plenty of dates, too, but when it came to attending the date itself, more often than not I bombed.

One woman with whom I matched on *Tinder*, a local nurse, invited me over to her apartment for sex one evening. I showed up at the appointed time, eager to do the deed. She answered the door dressed in tight jeans and an equally tight shirt that augmented her large bosoms. She was blonde, curvaceous, though a little on the butch side. I wasn't bothered by the latter.

I sat in a plush armchair opposite her, patting her elderly pet terrier, Gus, while she detailed the history of her miserable love life. She was still sore about her ex. He was a nurse like herself and apparently well-respected in his profession. She'd dated the guy for several years before getting engaged to him, only to discover, just months before the wedding, that her fiancée had been harbouring a profound secret: he was gay.

Like a good little simp, I excelled at the role of emotional tampon, listening attentively to her woes and offering my commiserations. Many women have a victim mentality and a compelling narrative, usually involving a man, to support their perceived status as a victim. Here was a perfect example of a woman who not only considered herself a victim, but who proudly wore her identity as a victim on her sleeve. I genuinely felt sorry for her; she was a mess. But there were other concerns on my mind—namely, whether I'd be getting laid tonight.

When I tried to lead the conversation in a sexual direction, she stated in a roundabout kind of way that she didn't find me attractive on account of my height (I was slightly shorter than her). Besides, she added, she was having a casual relationship with a lawyer, whom she'd met, like me, on *Tinder*. The guy was a bit of a player; he'd been seeing other women besides her. Yet she felt confident that, very soon, he'd finally be in a position to commit to her.

Without so much as offering me a glass of water, she began to make herself dinner. I continued to pat Gus, now curled up in a ball beside me. It was one of those dogs so old that the thing seemed to be rapidly decomposing—snotty nosed, watery eyed, given to wheezing loudly and emitting the occasional fart. I'd been rejected by the owner but not her dog. The dog, however, I did not wish to get too intimate with.

Her dinner now ready, she indicated that, given the lateness of the hour, I ought to be getting home. "Drive safe," she said as she ushered me out the door, closing it quickly behind me.

When a man goes on countless dates with women and consistently gets rejected, it sets him on a journey of self-discovery. Initially he goes through a period of anger and denial where he blames the female sex, convinced that *all* women are cold, stuck-up bitches, or that he's simply meeting the wrong kinds of women. Eventually, if he's mature and responsible enough, he comes to realise that he's part of the problem, and that, if he wants to succeed in the dating game, then he needs to get his shit together. Brutal self-honesty leads to the realisation that he's not as attractive or as wonderful as he thought he was. What follows is a commitment towards self-improvement.

I hadn't yet reached the self-improvement stage of my journey. Nor was I aware of my status as a simp. These breakthroughs would come much later. I had, however, taken a decent swig or two of brutal self-honesty and the taste was bitter and unpleasant on my tongue. For instance, I was aware why I was rarely getting second dates or indeed getting laid: it came down to a lack of confidence on my part. When out on a date with a woman I found attractive, I was an absolute wreck—needy, self-conscious, anxious, passive, awkward. My social and financial status wasn't much to rave about either.

These and other shortcomings of mine were inhibiting me from achieving success at online dating. Yet I was also aware—and I say this not to shift the blame, but rather for the sake of balance—that online dating tends to attract a certain "breed" of woman.

Generally speaking, these women are surrounded by drama, usually involving a guy with whom they're currently on the outs. They're "fixer-uppers": high-maintenance females with tons of emotional baggage and a high notch count. What's more, not all of them are seeking a relationship per se. Very often their motive for using online dating is to obtain validation and approval from men.

I was shocked by the number of women who, like Marie, weren't technically single. Secretly they already had boyfriends, yet because the relationship was going through a rough patch and they didn't want to end up single and alone, even for a moment, they'd turned to online dating to line up "Mr Plan B."

Of course, the depressing truth of online dating wouldn't dawn on me until roughly a year later. I remained convinced that online dating was the solution to my romantic and sexual woes; and so I kept at it, optimistic I'd finally meet the woman of my dreams.

For a period of about three months, I maintained a long-distance online relationship with a woman who lived in Hobart. Due to a temporary glitch with the app, we matched on *Tinder*, despite living hundreds of kilometres apart. We messaged each other multiple times a day, discussing our respective lives and interests in detail.

She was a marine engineer who'd spent years working at sea on cargo ships and other vessels. Not surprisingly for a woman employed in a male dominated profession, she described herself as "one of the boys," and hinted that, in her youth, she'd been intimate with more than a few of her male colleagues, mostly older men. In her own words, she "enjoyed a bit of vintage."

One night, while drunk, she called me on the phone. Her voice was odd—high-pitched, a little raspy; I inferred she'd been through the relationship wringer and was now barely holding it together. When, a few weeks later, we finally met in person, in a bakery situated in a tired, rural town half-way between her location and mine, matters fell flat. She looked nothing like the pretty, vibrant woman in her photos. Worse, the conversation strained like a wire brush against a rusty surface. The illusion suddenly broken, we immediately ceased messaging each other.

I decided it was time to change tactics. Clearly internet dating wasn't the solution. I would delete all of the dating apps on my phone and try to meet women in the real world instead. Just as I was about to go through with my plan, however, something unexpected happened: a young, tall, blonde woman, named Sarah, whom I'd matched with on *Tinder*, messaged to say that she'd like to meet up for a drink.

As I prepared for my date with Sarah, it was with the expectation that she'd be an absolute mess and the date a failure, so thoroughly disillusioned had I become with women in general and the internet dating scene in particular. I dressed simply, in a flannel shirt and jeans. My beard was getting a little on the unkempt side, but why trim it, I thought? Why bother making an effort?

When I arrived at the pub, Sarah was already waiting for me. She stood with arms and legs crossed, wearing a bashful smile. Her white skirt and emerald green cardigan matched the creamy tone of her skin. She was a good foot taller than me. The difference in height we'd already discussed and she said it didn't bother her. I was suspicious. It had been a deal breaker with every other tall woman I'd met online. Why not with Sarah? What was the catch?

The bar was loud and chaotic, packed with rowdy hillbilly couples: the women short, rotund, covered in unfashionable leg tattoos; the men bearded, heavily potbellied, fat fingered, and dressed in crusty work attire. Several members of a cricket team sat in the corner on stools, knocking back beers with gusto, as though worried the taps would run dry. Insufferable 90s hits blared over the speakers.

Not an ideal location for a first date, but we were here now, and it would have to do. We managed to find a vacant booth at the back, where it was just quiet enough to hold a conversation. I paid for the drinks.

I knew there was no way that Sarah would sleep with me; she was out of my league. Having already accepted this fact, I allowed myself to enjoy her company, letting her do most of the talking. She was only 23, a recent university graduate from South Australia.

A lover of camping, hiking and the outdoors, she'd
come to Tasmania to seek adventure and secure casual
employment.

Since joining *Tinder*, she explained, she'd received
no shortage of male attention. So far, though, she was
unimpressed with the quality of men available in the
local dating pool. They weren't sophisticated or intelligent enough, she said. Most of them talked about cars
and sport, whereas she appreciated art, music and for-
eign films. I was tempted to remind her that this was
rural Tasmania—not exactly a cultural Mecca—but I
wisely held my tongue.

Gradually the conversation drifted to politics. Don-
ald Trump was briefly discussed. She was, of course,
not a fan of the then US President, calling him a fascist
and a narcissist. Oddly, this was the third or fourth
date I'd been on in which Trump came up during conversation; women, it seemed, considered him the very
epitome of evil. Though I've never had a strong opinion
about Trump either way, I dared not say so. I agreed
he was a terrible human being and the worst thing to
happen to the human race ever.

Sarah, who'd majored in ecology at university, went
on to voice her support of feminism, socialism, LGBTQ
rights, the eradication of "rape culture," climate change
reversal, and other left-wing causes. Her political lean-
ings didn't surprise me in the least. Since entering the
dating scene, it had quickly come to my attention that
there exists among the female population a distinct
left-wing bias. As a "a white cis male" I was not to question these "progressive" narratives. Otherwise, I'd be
automatically perceived as a misogynist, a chauvinist,
a sexist, a transphobe, possibly even a racist, and rejection would be inevitable.

I gave Sarah the impression that I was on board

with her political views, as I was no doubt expected to be, then wisely steered the conversation to more personal, less divisive matters. She was extremely open about relationships and sex; and since I wasn't strongly invested in the outcome of the date, having already concluded that rejection was inevitable, I figured I may as well go balls out, caution be damned, while the moment was ripe and the alcohol flowing.

"You ought to tell me more about your *Tinder* dates," I said. "I'm intrigued."

She wrinkled her nose in disgust and disappointment. "It's been a mixed bag. I went on a couple of dates with a guy recently. He was okay to begin with. But he got super needy really quickly."

"Super needy how?"

"He texted me, like, five times a day, and when I didn't reply immediately, he'd text me again."

"That does sound a little desperate," I agreed.

"I told him we could be friends. After that he started acting weird. He sent me all these creepy messages about his dick. In the end I had to block him."

This, clearly, was unattractive behaviour on the guy's part. She was right to reject him, I thought. Though desperate myself, I hadn't yet sunk so low as to bring up the topic of my dick in the hope that a woman would want to sleep with me. I did wonder, though: had other girls considered my behaviour or intentions towards them creepy and weird? Probably.

Noticing myself leaning forwards too much, I corrected my posture, so that my back was now pressed against the seat. I'd read in a book about dating skills that leaning towards a woman during a date was not, as many men believed, an effective way to generate intimacy and connection, often having the precise opposite effect to that intended. It was recommended, instead, to lean backwards. This would prompt the woman to lean towards you. It was counterintuitive, but that's because women are like cats, explained the author. If you want to pat a cat, you need to let it come to you.

The advice in the book seemed to help: suddenly Sarah leaned towards me, reducing the space between us.

In a facetious tone I asked, "So you're looking for a guy who likes French movies and doesn't send you dick pics?"

She was quiet a moment as she gazed at her beer. "Actually, I'm not looking for a partner. I've already got one. I'm polyamorous."

I'd suspected from the beginning that there must be a catch. This was it: the girl fucked around with multiple guys. Part of me was tempted to roll my eyes, say "see you later" and walk straight out. Another, more persistent part of me was determined to stick around and see this through, if for no other reason than sheer entertainment value. Finally I'd encountered a poly-amorist. I was lost for words. The best I managed was "Wow."

"It's not something I advertise on my dating profile," she laughed. "Some guys are turned off by it initially."

No wonder. It didn't exactly turn me on either. What man in his right mind would want to share his girlfriend with another dude? I didn't say this, though. Rather I said, "It's unique. But each to their own. So how many guys are you, er, involved with?"

"Only three at this point."

Only three, I thought? Gosh, that's hardly any. You're fucking *only* three guys.

How she became involved in the poly lifestyle deserves explanation. She'd come to Tasmania not alone but with her boyfriend. They'd dated at university and were very much in love. It was to him that she'd lost her virginity. Aware of the sexual opportunities available to her as an attractive young woman no longer confined by the university bubble, she decided to discuss with her boyfriend an idea she'd been considering: *Why don't we both explore a little, with other people? Nothing emotional, just sex. So long as we keep each other informed of who's sleeping with whom, everything should work out fine.* The boyfriend agreed, so they both created profiles on *Tinder*.

Very quickly she started getting dates. Within the space of about a month, she'd acquired two fuck buddies: one a musician in his late-twenties who suffered from clinical depression; the other an outgoing builder in his thirties. With her partner's permission, she saw both men on a regular basis. In fact, the four of them had become good friends. They even spent weekends together camping, fishing, smoking weed, and generally just hanging out. There was no jealousy or competitiveness between her lovers, she insisted; they were just three dudes who enjoyed each other's company and who happened to be banging the same woman— namely, her. She saw nothing odd in this.

There was, however, one problem: her partner had failed to achieve the same level of success as her in the realm of online dating. In fact, not even close. Though he'd been on a few *Tinder* dates, none of them had led to sex. This, understandably, caused friction in their relationship. He was resentful that his girlfriend was getting lots of sex with other men and he none at all with other women.

He must have felt like an idiot for agreeing to an arrangement that was supposed to enhance his sex life, only to receive, instead of more pussy, the short end of the stick.

In the dating market, woman have a definite advantage over men, so her partner's lack of success wasn't necessarily through any fault of his own. She described him as well-spoken, confident, and reasonably good-looking. Not a single woman on *Tinder* had wanted to fuck him, though. I couldn't help but feel sorry for the guy. It was clear to me that, like myself, he was a complete and utter simp.

At that point I said something to Sarah which still surprises me for its brashness: "So you're absolutely sure that your boyfriend's okay with us sleeping together?"

Charmed, she replied with a smile, "I don't think that would be a problem."

I suggested that we go to my place, located just a short walk from the pub. She agreed without hesitation. Twenty minutes later we were making out at my apartment. Kissing escalated to fondling and very soon garments were removed. Her skin was hot, creamy and smooth, and already she was lubricated. It took me twenty minutes to make her come. Afterwards, I asked her if she wanted to stay the night but she politely declined; it went against one of the rules she'd established with her partner: no sleepovers.

It was the first time I'd had sex in well over a year and I couldn't believe my luck. Yet the encounter left me feeling unsatisfied, as though I'd had the appetiser but missed out on the main course. I'd tried so hard to please her so that she'd want to have sex with me again that I hadn't allowed myself to relax and fully enjoy the experience.

Simps are desperate, needy individuals, possessed of little self-respect and willing to degrade themselves for the precious, sacred booty. Once he notices a woman showing interest in him, he latches on like a tick. She becomes his nourishment. If she sleeps with him, he loses his mind altogether. He thinks he's found God between her thighs. Now she's more than nourishment; she's the centre of his universe, his salvation, his everything. Hallelujah.

Sarah was semi-nomadic and difficult to get in touch with, sometimes taking an entire month to reply to a single text message. It quickly became apparent that I wasn't a priority in her life.

Eventually she agreed on a second date, coming over to my house for dinner one night. I made beef curry and she brought along a bottle of wine. She was sexily dressed, in jeans and a low-cut shirt that revealed her generous cleavage. After dinner, we listened to music and made out. Things seemed to be going smoothly until it came to the moment I'd been waiting for. She wasn't in the mood for sex, she explained. Was it okay if we talked instead?

Somehow, during the course of the evening, I'd killed the mood. Not till after she'd gone home did it dawn on me how: I'd come across as desperate, needy, nervous, and eager to please. Unlike during the first encounter in which I hadn't particularly cared which way the evening would go, on this occasion I'd tried to force the date in a certain direction, which is hardly a way to charm a lady and inspire her to remove her pants.

The metaphor of women as cats springs to mind. Just as you can't force a cat to want to get patted, so you can't contrive a date with the expectation that the woman will want to fuck your brains out at the end of the evening. That's what hookers are for.

Besides, it's not as though Sarah was lacking for male company—she already had three men in her life with whom she was having sex on a regular basis. Why would she need a fourth? With me she'd increased her notch count by one. That accomplished, I was of little further use to her, apart from providing her with the occasional bit of company on those occasions when the other guys were unavailable or too busy to spend time with her or perhaps resentful over the fact that she'd been enthusiastically banging other men.

Having witnessed via my brief association with Sarah the desperate compromises men will make for female intimacy, myself included, I was left feeling thoroughly demoralised. She was pretty but by no means a stunner, and yet she had four men in her life willing to do anything to fuck her, each guy fully aware that she was simultaneously being fucked by every other guy. Form an orderly queue, boys!

Clearly, I wasn't the only simp. Most men, as far as I could gather, were simps these days. Ours was a generation of simps. We are fucking pathetic.

Traditionally, men were the ones who dominated the sexual marketplace and benefited from polyamory, who, if wealthy enough, had multiple wives, kept mistresses, and so forth. Now the shoe was on the other foot. Women had all the power. Dating apps, in particular, had changed the game. By means a of a smart phone, a woman could create a *Tinder* profile with the press of a few keys on her phone and be riding the cock carousel by sundown.

Even if, after enjoying all that cock, she decided she wanted to commit to a serious, exclusive relationship with a man, she'd still be spoilt for choice, with plenty of desperate guys lining up to take on the role. It didn't matter if she'd sucked more cock than a 70s porn star. Nor did it matter if she was a single mum with five kids by three different fathers. Such is the overinflated value of the booty in our now female-centric society. Meanwhile, there are untold numbers of men, deemed low value by women, who remain excluded from the sexual marketplace, some destined to remain virgins their whole lives.

My experience with Sarah was disheartening but ultimately eye-opening. Tired of the drama of online dating and the stresses and hassles associated with women in general, I figured there must be a more effective way to get laid, one that didn't exact such a high psychological price. It was this realisation that prompted me to contact the Asian prostitute.

Once inside the hotel lobby, I paused to gather my bearings. The place reeked of neglect and poor taste. The air was stale, dusty, catching at the back of my throat; I suppressed the urge to cough. Uninspired Australiana-themed paintings adorned cracked beige walls. My shoes sunk into carpet so worn I doubt it had ever been replaced.

The desk at reception was unattended, thank god. I didn't want to be seen, least of all identified as the client of a hooker. Apart from the occasional snippet of conversation emanating from the distant bar, there was little evidence of human activity. Clearly not a busy night at the hotel. But, then, was it ever busy at this shithole?

I located room 22 at the very end of the second-floor hallway. Here I paused, heart beating loudly in my chest, palms sweaty. I knew it would be cowardly to bail now, seeing as I'd already come this far. No, I reminded myself, I had to go through with my mission. Fortune favours the bold. It's also the bold who get laid.

I reached forward in preparation to knock when my ears registered the sound of animated talking from behind the door. Two women. Possibly speaking Mandarin. But why two? Finally, with weak knees and a trembling fist, I forced myself to knock. Seconds later the door creaked open to reveal a face peering back at me, goblin-like, from within a dimly lit entrance. "Come in," she beckoned.

I stepped through the threshold, mentally crossing my fingers for good luck and protection. Instantly my nostrils were assaulted by the thick, oily stench of cheap Asian takeaway. The place was spacious, a suite as opposed to a bedsit. It had its own kitchenette at the back, the benchtop littered with brightly-coloured fast-food packaging.

My host quickly shut the door behind me, then motioned me to a room off to the side. The second woman I couldn't see.

"Are you Tina?" I asked, hoping to hell that she wasn't.

She was short, barely five feet, aged in her forties, if not older, and hardly a likely contender for the hot Asian hooker award. Her breasts were saggy and flat and her belly exhibited a noticeable bulge. A cream-coloured nightgown hung from her tired, worn figure.

"Yes," she answered with an insincere smile. "I'm Tina. I show you good time. You bring money?"

I wanted to scream loudly, then die. This was not the Tina I'd expected. Clearly a case of false advertising. I'd been fucking duped.

"You bring money?" she repeated.

My wallet was in my trouser pocket. I'd noticed her greedily eyeing the area ever since I'd entered. She was determined to be paid, no matter what.

"I have the money, yes, but I was expecting a much

younger woman." I immediately regretted using the word "younger"; I had no intention of offending the woman.

She cracked a mischievous smile and, leaning forward, tapped me on the crotch of my trousers, right on the tip of my now shrunken cock. I jumped back in repulsion, holding my hands in the air in mock surrender. The woman was crazy, a real wildcat.

Tina, frustrated by my stubbornness but committed to winning me over, took a step closer. "Come on, baby," she goaded. "I put you in my mouth. Just $50."

I briefly considered the offer, if for no other reason than to get her off my back. But the thought of receiving a blow job from those lips—lips that, no doubt, had touched many an unwashed trucker's cock—disgusted me. To say nothing of how I would fake an erection were she to actually go through with the act.

"I appreciate the offer," I lied. "But I've changed my mind. Sorry."

She nodded. "Wait here. I come back."

I felt like a prisoner. Would Tina allow me to leave without being paid first? I doubted it. Most likely she'd demand payment, regardless of my having declined her services.

Her brief absence gave me a chance to more fully inspect my prison cell. It was the very definition of unsavoury. Opposite the door was a rickety aluminium window, the kind that never closes properly, and below it an unmade bed fitted with plastic sheets. Near my feet was a wastepaper bin, filled to the brim with used tissues, and beside it an extra-large box of latex gloves.

It was then that I fully registered the smell, that of stale sweat and semen, the essence of male horniness run amok. If I allowed myself to puke, I'd probably never stop.

I heard Tina speak to the other woman in the suite, their conversation loud and rapid. I hadn't the foggiest idea what they were saying, yet it was apparent I'd upset the applecart, difficult client that I was. What did she plan to do with me? Have her friend in the other room "service" me instead?

Tina returned accompanied by her friend, an older, though slightly thinner and healthier-looking woman. Her friend was the first to speak. "You go now, if you like."

"Silly man," said Tina, shaking her head. "Don't come back."

As soon as her friend opened the door, I bolted into the hallway like a frightened foal. In my panic-ridden state, I lost my bearings and failed to find the proper exit, so ended up leaving the building via the fire escape.

I obeyed Tina's words: I never went back.

The old man has been laughing for a minute so far, cackling his head off like a lunatic. Finally, he stops, catches his breath and says, "Boy did those Asian hookers pull the wool over your eyes. A sexy young student, indeed."

"I guess it's funny," I admit, "but at the time it wasn't. She was ugly as hell, and I was terrified. I honestly wasn't sure I'd escape."

He shrugs, still red in the face from laughing. "Live and learn, eh?"

"Sounds like you're speaking from experience," I quip.

"I've shagged my fair share of whores, sure. Three in Thailand. Two in Eastern Europe. Not to mention all the women I've dated who ultimately turned out to be whores."

"You mean actual whores or metaphorical whores?"

"What's the difference?"

"The vast majority of low-quality women are whores to varying degrees by virtue of the fact that they expect money and resources in exchange for putting out. Either they want actual money or they want your energy, validation, attention, or—heck—your skills as a handy man. Most of them aren't even aware that they're whores, to such a degree have they internalised their whoredom."

"If you mean that women are whores because they expect men to provide for them, then I guess you're right, they're whores. Men are traditionally providers. That's the way it's always been. We hunt—or used to. We build houses, skyscrapers, bridges. Work on oilrigs. Put in long hours at the office. All to support women and children."

"That's partly true," says the old man, "but I'm not saying all woman are whores. I'm saying certain low-quality women are whores." He thinks for a moment before adding, "What's the name of that dating site you joined?"

"*Tinder*?"

"No. The other one."

"*Plenty of Fish*."

"Ah, yes, *Plenty of Fish*. Attracting a woman into your life is much like fishing. You need to be careful where you cast your line and what you bait it with. If the water's polluted, stagnant and the bait's no good or the wrong kind, the chance you'll reel in a delicious healthy fish is virtually nil. Then there are the sharks to watch out for."

"Sharks? Really? I didn't encounter any of those."

"Yes, you did, only you were fortunate not to get eaten. Take Marie, for example. Had her ex-boyfriend not come back into the picture, it's likely you would've fallen into her trap, especially if she'd been a good fuck. When you date a single mother, not only are you required to spend all of your free time with her, you're also expected to play the role of surrogate dad to her kids. On top of that you're obliged to pay not just for her but for her kids as well. That's a huge investment of time, money, and energy. Marie would've chewed you up and spat you out, before moving onto the next gullible guy, probably within a week. Single mothers are the biggest whores you'll ever meet."

"Maybe," I say with a shrug. "They do come across as opportunistic. Lots of single mums on dating sites."

"And no wonder. How else but via internet dating are they able to snag a man?" Suddenly he leans forward and pats me on the shoulder. "I'm proud of you, son. You journeyed to the land of whores and survived!"

"I suppose," I reply, uncertain. "Although I did come close to sleeping with an actual whore."

"Oh, I wouldn't worry about her. She was the only whore in your story who possessed an ounce of integrity. Which is ironic, really, because she lied about her age and appearance. Still, at least you knew where you stood with that particular whore. It's the sneaky, ambiguous whores, the ones who advertise themselves on dating sites—they're the whores you need to be wary of."

There's a period of silence between us. Then the old man adds with a smile, "Tina the Asian hooker. Now there's a whore I would've fucked. Your loss, son."

4

SHE WAS NEVER YOURS; IT WAS JUST YOUR TURN

When you realise you're getting older and that time is your most precious asset, it opens your eyes to what's important in life. You begin to see your existence from a more elevated perspective, and with this knowledge comes the realisation that you can't afford to continue repeating the same mistakes, unless you're prepared to waste more time and endure more suffering. And who wants that?

I knew I had a choice: either I could stay a simp, making women the focus of my existence and getting absolutely nowhere, or I could focus on becoming a better version of myself. I chose the latter. Whether I'd achieve my goal would remain to be seen.

I was now in my mid-thirties, no longer young and brimming with energy, and it was apparent I was beginning to go bald. Whenever I combed my hair, loose strands would gather on the end of the comb. I was horrified. Baldness runs in my family, even affecting

my older brother, who consequently resembles Prince
William. I decided the only solution was to shave my
head. Better to have no hair at all, I figured, than to
end up looking like my dad or brother. One morning I
finally bit the bullet: using the electric clippers I shaved
my head clean.

The result wasn't as bad as I'd expected. Yet I wasn't
exactly enamoured with my new look either. Initially
I was embarrassed to leave the house without a hat,
worried what other people would think of me. Over
time I stopped caring, to the point where I was able to
walk down the street without being overly conscious of
my lack of hair. Eventually I bought a grey flat cap—not
to hide but rather to complement my baldness. I also
added to my wardrobe several pairs of new jeans, half-
a-dozen nice shirts, and a couple of stylish jackets.

When you begin taking pride in your appearance,
women pay attention. They notice not the clothes per
se, but the confident way you carry yourself as a well-
dressed man. Mark Twain was right when he said that
"Clothes make the man."

My improved appearance and newfound confidence
had an instant positive impact. Several women from
work started showing a romantic interest in me. Initially I paid little attention to their advances. For the
first time in a long while I was coasting along okay in
life. I was feeling optimistic, centred, goal-oriented.
The last thing I needed or wanted was the drama that
arises from being entangled with a woman.

For better or worse, my desire to get laid won out
over my desire to lead a peaceful life. Enter Rachel,
a short goth chick in her twenties with tits as big as
cantaloupes, a ring through her nose, bright purple
hair, and tattoos along her arms and across her shoulders and back. I occasionally sat next to her at work,

and before long we were chatting on a regular basis. That I possessed little genuine desire for the woman beyond wanting to satisfy my carnal urges only further increased her attraction towards me.

She was a strange creature. More accurately, she pretended to be strange for the sake of attracting attention. She dressed in eccentric outfits decorated with pictures of witches on broomsticks and flaming pumpkins—even when Halloween was months away. You could always hear her coming because she stomped around the office in chunky, lace-up boots. She was an unabashed slut. She flirted openly, her impressive cleavage on full display. Several guys in the office wanted to fuck her, and I dare say she'd already fucked a few of them by the time we met.

One day I received a message from her out of the blue, inviting me over to her house for an evening drink. I of course accepted, knowing it would probably lead to sex. She lived in a neighbouring town just a short drive away. I arrived at the appointed time to the sound of heavy metal tunes blasting through the door. The interior was dimly-lit, decorated with all the usual goth knick-knacks—statues of dragons, pictures of heavy metal singers, crystal orbs, pentagrams.

We sat in her kitchen drinking into the early hours of the evening. She consumed alcohol like a whore in a tavern and encouraged me to do the same. The moment I finished each beer, she'd hand me another one from the fridge. "Are you trying to get me drunk?" I asked her. Her response: "Yes and it seems to be working too."

When I returned from the bathroom, she finally pounced, kissing me on the mouth while reaching into my pants. She was an aggressive kisser; it felt as though my lips and tongue were being pulled off my face. The sex was okay, although it took her an extremely long time to come, requiring a huge amount of effort on my part. I was left feeling drained, as though I'd just been attacked by a succubus.

I dated Rachel for a period of six months, staying over at her house at least two nights a week for sex and occasionally dinner. We agreed to see each other exclusively, although it didn't take her long to break that rule.

When, after being involuntarily celibate for a year or so, you finally enter into a sexual relationship with a woman, the fact that you're getting laid is enough to cloud your judgement as to the true character of the woman in question. Your brain takes a back seat while your dick takes the wheel; and though it's fun to cruise around while the pussy's wet and there's plenty of jizz in the tank, your dick's not the most responsible driver. Eventually you wind up in a ghetto somewhere, broken down on the side of the road late at night.

Under all that make up, piercings, and ink, Rachel was hiding more than a few red flags. Daddy issues leaked from every pore of her body. When I asked her about the numerous thin scars along her arms, she explained that she'd purposely cut herself as a teenager. She'd since given up the cutting; her anxiety and depression she now managed with heavy doses of *Zoloft*.

After her parents split up when she was still just a toddler, her mother, a massage therapist and former go-go dancer from France, took on the role of raising her on her own. Her mother was as crazy as a cut snake and hated men with the intensity of a radical feminist at a women's march. She wasn't a cat lady but something much worse: a dog lady. She especially liked big dogs and insisted they were "better than men." She cohabited with several of the shaggy beasts, even sleeping in bed with them.

Rachel remained estranged from her father, whom she'd been taught to despise from a young age. She knew little about him, except that he'd worked as a truck driver; that he'd fathered many children by many different women; and that, partly to avoid paying child support, he'd retired to Thailand, marrying a succession of young Thai women.

Rachel hated men, too, though not quite to the same extent as her mother. Her first boyfriend, with whom she shared custody of a young daughter, she broke up with after he became too "needy." Countless relationships followed, with both male and female partners. She was the consummate party girl, forever sleeping around, too scared to commit to a single person and eager to keep her options open.

When we met, she'd just come out of a two-year relationship with a much older man, a former amphetamine user who'd since managed to clean up his life and find stable work as a handyman. She described him as a decent guy, in spite of his troubled past. He worked hard to support her and her daughter, happily took on the role of step-father to her daughter, and frequently showered her with gifts. He was extremely devoted to her, at one point proposing marriage.

She told me she broke up with him on account of his addiction to gaming; he gamed so much, apparently, that it got to the point where they barely communicated. Of course, I knew the real reason behind their breakup: Rachel wasn't long-term girlfriend material. The man, in his naivety, had tried to turn a whore into a housewife.

Women with daddy issues who are sexually promiscuous tend to get on better with men than members of their own gender. Rachel was no exception in this regard. She told me she enjoyed the company of guys; they were "laid back" and "easy to please." Women, on the other hand, she found "bitchy" and difficult to handle. Consequently, she had enough male friends to establish a sausage factory, but almost no female friends to speak of (except one or two very butch women). Whenever we spent time together, she'd continually be on her phone exchanging messages with dudes.

Her male friends were oddly protective towards her and critical of every guy she'd dated. By far her closest male friend, Gavin, whom she'd known since high school and whom she regarded, she said, as "an older brother," made it his duty to reply to every one of her *Facebook* posts, often in a sexually suggestive way.

I had the pleasure of meeting Gavin on his wedding day. Built like a giant, with arms and legs as thick as tree trunks, he looked as though he ate handfuls of meat pies for breakfast. The rest of his family members were just as large and muscular, including his 70-year-old grandmother. Strong, hillbilly stock. Plenty of brawn, but zero brains.

Earlier I'd been warned by Rachel that Gavin would try to psyche me out, and that's precisely what happened. Within minutes of being introduced to each other, he launched into a series of "jokes" about the times he used to fuck Rachel on the kitchen counter. While still reeling from the shock of his comments, he took me aside and told me in no uncertain terms that he'd beat me up if I ever harmed his friend.

Gavin and Rachel had a long and complicated history. Yet, according to her, not once had they slept together. They were simply good friends, nothing more. While she admitted he'd propositioned her several times during the more than ten years they'd known each other, on each of those occasions she'd turned him down. The reason: she didn't find him physically attractive.

I was well aware that Gavin, motivated by jealousy, was trying to drive a wedge between me and Rachel, and, consequently, that I ought to take his words with a bucket load of salt. At the same time, it struck me as highly unlikely that Rachel, given her long history of promiscuous behaviour, hadn't fucked him at least once, perhaps by mistake during a messy night of drinking. Generally, when one party is claiming one thing and the other party the opposite, the truth lies somewhere in the middle.

One night at her house, Rachel and I had a fight concerning Gavin, which ended in her launching a bottle of beer across the room. She threw it, fortunately, in the opposite direction to my head. It smashed against the wall, raining glass and foamy beer onto the tiles below. I was aware she had an angry streak but this was the first time I'd seen her express her anger physically.

Afterwards, our relationship remained on shaky ground. Out of fear of being dumped and ending up, once again, alone, a simp will do whatever he can to try and patch things up with a woman, even when it's glaringly obvious that the relationship isn't working. He'll bend over backwards to keep her in his life. The woman, sensing this, will perceive him as weak, desperate, needy, and ultimately unattractive, causing her to pull away.

As the weeks wore on, I heard from Rachel less and less. Our sexual encounters, though they still occurred, were infrequent. More often than not, she was "too busy" to see me. Worried she'd stop having sex with me altogether, I figured I needed to step up as a boyfriend and invest more time and energy into keeping her happy. To this end, I started showering her with money and favours: buying her dinners, mowing her lawn, walking her dog, playing frisbee with her daughter, vacuuming her house, and even doing her dishes.

My approach had the opposite effect to that intended, further compounding her view of me as a grovelling fool lacking value and self-worth. No wonder, too—becoming a woman's butler is hardly a way to communicate that you're a high value male.

I had a gut feeling she was sleeping with someone else, possibly one of her guy friends. My suspicion was confirmed about a week later when, one night before sex, she handed me a condom from the box located inside her bedside draw. After rolling it onto my cock, I noticed it felt different, not as tight. During sex, it kept sliding off. I was perplexed. It's not as though I wasn't erect.

After we'd finished and Rachel was occupied in the bathroom, I turned on the lamp to inspect the box of condoms, at which point the cause of the problem was revealed: they were extra-large, not the usual medium size. The box was half-empty, too—odd because I'd only used one.

That's the last time I ever saw Rachel. I never discovered who her new lover was. Yet, judging by the size of the condoms he wore, I can only assume he was hung like a shire stallion.

***

Every now and then, if you're not paying attention, a person will come into your life who, though ostensibly benevolent and well-intentioned, will wreak such havoc and destruction that, once it's all over and the dust and smoke has cleared, you'll be left with a greatly diminished view of humanity and the knowledge that you're not as smart, wise or discerning as you thought you were.

Such people, in my experience, are usually women.

I was still feeling rough as a consequence of my break up with Rachel. You don't need to be in love with a woman to suffer emotionally when the relationship ends. Knowing she'd been fucking another guy at the time we were still together made the experience sting just that little bit more.

It was in the midst of this low point in my life that KitKat made her appearance. Why she called herself KitKat I still have no idea. She possessed many nicknames and went by many different aliases; and though she provided a Florida address at the time I knew her, she had, she admitted, a tendency to move around a lot; she'd previously lived in Oregon, New Mexico and Texas, among other states.

As an author who used to write books on the science and mystery of sleep, I'm occasionally contacted by female readers who are, for want of a better term, groupies. They're flirtatious, hungry for attention, and shower me with flattery. Occasionally such a woman will send me an unsolicited photo of herself in a sexy pose, irrespective of whether she has a partner.

I knew straight away that KitKat was a groupie. She sent me a long, disjointed email in which she praised one of my books. Believing herself to be clairvoyant, she wanted to know if I'd care to read a description of her dream about Abraham Lincoln that left her feeling as though she'd been visited by the spirit of the long-deceased president. Out of politeness I said "yes." Naturally, her email smacked of narcissism and magical thinking. But, then, having received lots of strange emails over the years, I thought little of it. I replied politely thinking that was that.

My reply to her email prompted a further reply from her. Then, somehow, she found me on *Twitter*. Then *Facebook*. The messages came in thick and fast. I replied intermittently, depending on how busy I happened to be.

I was tempted to ignore her altogether when, one morning, I woke up to a message from her that instantly piqued my interest. It was easily the filthiest thing I'd ever been sent by a woman, and I mean that in the best way possible. She was a raging nymphomaniac. She pulled no punches. Even better, she'd attached a naked photo to accompany the message. Though a little on the blurry side, I could tell she had a nice body—large breasts, wide hips, a shapely ass.

More explicit photos and dirty messages followed. She was unstoppable, insatiable. All she had on her mind was sex. I was in internet pussy heaven. It was almost as good as, if not better than, having a physical woman in my life. I could jerk off to one of her messages then instantly go to sleep and not have to hear her drone on about her problems. Sexual gratification without all the drama.

Little did I know there'd be drama and lots of it—just not the kind of drama I was accustomed to with a woman.

Eventually she suggested we chat via *Skype*. She wanted to get to know me more intimately, she said. I was hesitant at first, worried the attraction might instantly vanish upon seeing each other via webcam. That I'd been catfished was a distinct possibility. What if she looked nothing like her photos? What if—god forbid—she was a man pretending to be a woman?

It turned out my concerns were unfounded. She was just as sexy and attractive on camera as she was in her photos; just as coquettish, too—she wasn't shy about flashing her tits or pulling down her sweatpants to show me her lacey panties. Her only unattractive feature was her voice. It was a little too singsongy and girly for my liking, hinting at a lack of sincerity, as though she were playing a role for my benefit. I attributed this to her obsession with Marilyn Monroe, with whom she identified closely. I wondered: was she trying to emulate Monroe because she lacked a firm identity herself?

The *Skype* conversations continued. Though sometimes difficult to schedule given that we lived in separate continents, with my mornings being her evenings and vice versa, we managed to make it work. That she tended to sleep during the day and stay up all night meant we were often free at the same time. She wasn't exactly time poor either. Apart from looking after her teenage daughter, she had few responsibilities. She didn't have a job but relied on welfare.

Never before had I met a woman so sexually uninhibited. The webcam sex was primarily her idea, and she couldn't seem to get enough of it. Each time we spoke on *Skype*, she'd immediately take off her clothes, then, after a bit of mutual dirty talk, she'd go all out, adopting various poses while she pleasured herself with a vibrator.

She enjoyed seeing me naked as well. She was a huge fan of the cum-shot, and countless towels were dirtied in the process of satisfying her in this regard. Though initially camera shy and unable to get fully hard, I quickly gained confidence, spraying my load like a porn star while she moaned loudly and offered words of encouragement.

She was skilled at dirty talk, capable of making me hard with her words alone, but sometimes she'd let slip a remark so bizarre that it would temporarily throw me off my game. People say some weird shit in the heat of the moment, like the time I told a woman that I wanted to fuck her tits and her pussy simultaneously (clearly impossible, unless you have two penises). This, however, was on a whole other level of weirdness. "Fuck me with your dolphin," she once yelled just before coming. That one spun me out. Just as strange were her use of the terms "spunk" and "gush." She wanted to feel my "spunk" "gush" all over her body, she said.

When you start to become more comfortable with a woman and the sexual thrill wears off to some extent, partly because she no longer perceives you as mysterious, that's when the reality of the relationship reveals itself. You begin to discern cracks; then the cracks widen, become bigger, until finally the whole ceiling caves in, falling down on top of you.

Women, though they enjoy sex for purely biological reasons, generally aren't sexual with men for this reason alone. They have a bigger goal in mind. Sex for a woman is always transactional. A woman will meet your sexual needs so long as you provide her with something in return. With respect to KitKat, the sex most certainly wasn't free. She had, it turned out, a great deal of baggage from the past that she wanted to get off her chest, and I, unable to put up healthy boundaries, quickly became her emotional tampon.

The flow, once it started, didn't end. One night, having failed to place my phone on silent before going to sleep, I was awakened by a stream of dings. They were messages from KitKat, about thirty in total, pertaining to her screwed up childhood; the abuse she'd suffered at the hands of men she'd dated in the past; along with random conspiracy stuff about shape-shifting reptilian aliens running the world and how there was a secret plot within Hollywood to replace female actors with transwomen.

I was able to forgive her for the nocturnal messages—she lived, after all, in a different time zone—but I politely suggested that, instead of messaging me so much, she wait until the next *Skype* call. This pissed her off, but she nonetheless complied. At least for a couple of nights. She was convinced we were officially dating at this point and felt, as a girlfriend would, entitled to my constant, unwavering attention.

I went along with the notion of being her boyfriend, even adding her on *Facebook* and updating my profile to "in a relationship" because she demanded that I do so. I figured it would make her happy, so why not? She proved to be the jealous sort, however, and I very quickly regretted my decision.

One morning I awoke to a stream of angry messages about how I was cheating on her and what a piece of shit I was. It turns out she'd gone through my *Facebook* friends list and, upon noticing that a certain attractive young woman had liked a few of my posts, had immediately assumed that the woman and I were engaged in a wild sexual relationship. The real explanation wasn't quite so dramatic: the young woman was my sixteen-year-old niece.

KitKat offered a sincere apology, and we quickly put the matter behind us. She confessed that she struggled with feelings of insecurity as a consequence of being cheated on in the past. I assured her I wasn't going to cheat on her, promising exclusivity in the relationship.

"You're different to other guys," she replied. "I can tell you really care. I can't help but wonder if we're soul mates or something."

The *Skype* sex was still ongoing at this point, though less frequently so, in part because she'd become insecure about certain aspects of her body. She was born with large labia, she revealed, and although, at the age of twenty, she'd undergone a gynoplasty to correct this, she'd never felt entirely confident about the appearance of her "muffin," as she called it. Much to my frustration, I continually had to assure her that her "muffin" was attractive and desirable.

One evening she announced that she wanted to place more emphasis on conversation and connection than sex. Supporting her desire to deepen the relationship, I encouraged her, to my instant regret, to share with me more about her past and upbringing. What followed was a detailed account of her entire life story.

She hated her parents, calling them "goblins." Her mother was a hoarder and crazy cat lady and her father a compulsive nose-picker and sexual deviant who'd once penned a book about his love of being spanked as a child. While growing up, the family moved around a lot on account of her father's job as a United Nations officer, spending time in Turkey, Afghanistan, Pakistan and other countries throughout the Middle East.

Her parents, though not explicitly abusive towards her, damaged her with neglect. At the age of seven, she fantasised about killing them as they slept, planning the crime in detail in her head. She imagined dousing their bed in petrol and setting fire to it with a match. She took great pleasure, she told me, in the thought of watching them burn to death while screaming their heads off. When I expressed the view that murder was morally wrong, she merely shrugged and replied that some people deserved to die.

At the age of fifteen, her parents' marriage collapsed and she ended up living with her mother. As a consequence of her mother's penchant for hoarding, bags of reeking garbage lined the hallways of the house, making it a squeeze to get out the front door. Rats, roaches and silverfish, attracted to the garbage, were a constant problem, though her mother's cats took care of the former.

Eager to escape, she moved out at the age of seventeen to live with her boyfriend at the time, an alcoholic in his late-thirties with a troubled past. Their relationship was a roller-coaster ride of partying, drinking, amphetamine use, loud and dramatic fights, breaking up and making up. She eventually fell pregnant by him, giving birth to a daughter. When her daughter was only three, the father was found dead of alcohol abuse. It was KitKat's belief that she'd killed him using her "occult powers." She was a witch, she told me proudly, and when she cursed someone, either intentionally or unintentionally, their life would fall apart and they'd meet some tragic end.

KitKat shared with me further crazy stories from her past, the nostalgia thick in her voice and evident in her eyes. Most of these stories concerned drug-fuelled adventures she'd had with friends while living in Europe as a rebellious young woman. Though she'd tried—and enjoyed—just about every drug imaginable, including LSD and peyote, her greatest love was—and remained—alcohol.

Hers was a chequered past, yet her current existence didn't sound a whole lot better. It was evident that she still hit the bottle hard. She confessed she had a tendency to act recklessly and impulsively while drunk, sometimes passing out and losing her memory of recent events and occasionally waking up in the beds of strangers.

A weakness for drugs and alcohol is one thing. Sexual promiscuity is another. Very often, though, the two overlap. When she casually mentioned she'd dated her fair share of men, I told her that, for my own peace of mind, I preferred not to know her precise body count.

Wanting to get it off her chest, she told me anyway.

One night, out of the blue, she emailed me a list of every guy she'd ever slept with. There were almost sixty names in total. While some were nothing more than one-night stands, the vast majority were actual relationships. I gathered she wasn't so much a slut as she was a serial monogamist. Each relationship had been a complete disaster—brief, stormy, and conflict-ridden—leading her to conclude that the guy had been an asshole and she the helpless victim.

I wasn't sure what to make of her serial monogamy but for the most part I accepted her explanation that she'd been "unlucky in love." Over time, as the stories she shared about herself became more and more wild and her behaviour increasingly unstable and bizarre, I found myself questioning her character and integrity. Later I would come to conclude that she suffered from borderline personality disorder.

It came as something of a bombshell when, one evening, she revealed she had a criminal record. She'd been to gaol twice in the past, showing me the mugshots to prove it. Her first stint occurred in relation to an incident where she crashed her car into a highway guardrail while her daughter—at the time a young child—was in the backseat; the second in relation to a domestic dispute between her and her sister that became physically violent.

She insisted that neither incident was her fault and provided excuses for both. It wasn't intoxication or speeding that led to her crashing her car; it was because she'd "passed out" after taking a sip of *Coke*. As for the domestic dispute, her sister was the instigator and hence entirely to blame.

We'd been chatting online for a couple of months, becoming increasingly intimate in the process, when she expressed her love for me and a desire that we one day get married. Initially I was speechless, not sure how to take the news. It was too early to be talking about love and marriage, never mind the fact that our relationship was extremely long distance and entirely online, such that we'd probably never meet in person, let alone get married. These thoughts, of course, I kept to myself. I told her I loved her too, just to make her happy.

Despite her chequered past, I felt, deep down, that she was fundamentally a good person. I regarded her the way I regarded a used car with many miles on the odometer: potentially in need of frequent maintenance but good value for the price. Besides, I was happy to be her "mechanic." It was a role I'd embraced with all my previous "fixer-upper" girlfriends. I was good at helping women, I told myself. Unlike most other men, I was sensitive, caring, a good listener, and capable of providing unconditional love and support.

At the time I believed that even the most damaged people could be fixed; and since I further believed that women are fundamentally better than men—kinder, gentler, more "spiritual"—it seemed self-evident to me that they were the ones most deserving of society's love and support.

During one of our regular *Skype* conversations, KitKat proposed an exciting idea: that I visit her at her home in Florida for a couple of weeks. She longed to meet me in person. Yes, she admitted, she'd dated a lot of guys, but I was the guy she truly wanted, the one she'd been searching for her entire life, perhaps even her soulmate. So profound was our connection, she believed, that we'd first met in a previous incarnation.

If I came to see her, she'd make sure I had the trip of a lifetime. We'd have amazing sex at least three times a

day, go for walks along beautiful beaches, and visit all
the local attractions. Mostly, though, we'd have amazing sex. She'd already purchased some sexy lingerie
that she planned to wear for me. She liked it rough,
dirty, and intense. She'd wake me up every morning
with a blowjob, she said, then demand that I take her
from behind. And would I please "gush" my "spunk" all
over her "muffin" and tits?

The decision was easy to make. I hadn't had sex in
over six months. I was horny as hell and eager to get
my dick wet. And maybe, just maybe, the relationship
was "meant to be." Perhaps we'd fall in love, get married, and I'd end up living with her and her daughter
in Florida. Even if, upon meeting face-to-face, the
attraction between us was to suddenly vanish and no
physical relationship ensue, at least I'd get to have an
exciting holiday in a country I'd never visited before.
It was win-win either way. The tickets were expensive,
but why the hell not? Life is short. Be bold!

Figuring out how to fly from Tasmania to Florida the cheapest and most direct way possible was a
nightmare, requiring a trip to the local travel agent,
plus many hours of internet research. To save money,
I ended up making the booking myself. It was an ex-
travagant purchase, to say the least, and in a way I felt
like a fool for parting with so much money, especially
given the element of risk involved. But mostly I was
excited—and relieved—that I'd gone through with it.

I immediately notified KitKat by email, attaching a
copy of the ticket for confirmation. I then waited for her
response. And waited. Normally she replied straight
away. What was keeping her this time, I wondered?

She didn't respond until the following afternoon.
Her message was terse, matter of fact. She said she was
"happy" I'd decided to book my ticket and that she was

"looking forward to meeting me in person." It wasn't quite the declaration of enthusiasm I'd expected.

That evening, while chatting on *Skype*, we had an argument. Somehow, during the course of the discussion, the topic of her body count arose. Deep down she knew that I wasn't entirely comfortable with her promiscuity. The first time she'd brought it up, I'd chosen my words carefully, worried I might say something offensive. On this occasion, I spoke out of turn.

"I guess it's a little on the high side," I said. "Perhaps a bit higher than that of most women."

As a way to lighten the mood, I delivered the comment accompanied by a chuckle. It was a stupid thing to say and I regretted it immediately. I tried to back pedal, saying I didn't mean it, but by that stage it was already too late. Furious at having been, according to her, "slut shamed," she immediately hung up. Straight away she blocked me on *Facebook*.

I sent her a long email in which I poured out my heart and begged for forgiveness. Two days later she replied, saying I'd hurt her so deeply, that I'd caused such terrible harm to the relationship, that it was over between us. She urged me to refund my ticket. She didn't want to speak to me ever again. To visit her in Florida was out of the question.

In the days that followed, I was consumed with anger, both towards myself and KitKat. I'd spent nearly $2000 on an airline ticket to visit a woman in a foreign country, a woman I'd met on the internet and barely knew, and now she no longer wanted me to visit her. All because of something stupid I'd said that triggered her insecurities around being a slut. Her insecurities were her own, yet I was supposed to take the blame for them. The bitch had led me on, and I, being a pathetic, dick-thinking simp, had fallen for it. Was I a fucking moron? Had I learned nothing in all my years of deal-ing with unstable women?

I spend a week panicking, not knowing what the fuck to do. Should I go ahead with the trip and book myself into a hotel for the duration of my stay? Or should I cancel it altogether and request a refund on the ticket? In the end I chose the latter. Relief washed over me the moment I was told I'd be getting back 85% of the purchase price—more than I'd anticipated.

Soon after making the cancellation, KitKat started messaging me again. She said I was now forgiven and that she loved and missed me. She urged me to go ahead and book another flight, saying she'd make it up to me with lots of amazing sex in Florida. I told her I no longer trusted her and that we ought to go our separate ways. This she refused to accept.

The more I ignored her messages, the more per-sistently she pursued me. Almost every day for the next couple of weeks, I'd wake up to twenty or thirty messages on my phone. The first few messages would be friendly and desperate—for example, "I miss you, please forgive me!"—only to become meaner and cra-zier with each succeeding message, finally ending with something along the lines of, "I think you're a piece of shit and I hope you die alone, motherfucker!"

After blocking her on *Facebook*, she started filling up my email inbox. It was the same pattern of friendly, desperate messages—sometimes including naked pho-tos—followed by progressively nasty messages. Never before had I encountered a woman so unstable, so chaotic, so easily able to fluctuate between cutesy se-ductress one minute and raging bitch the next. She was relentless, persistent, obsessed, more demonic than human. It occurred to me I'd dodged a bullet by being forced to cancel my ticket. Had I travelled to Florida to see her, I doubt I would've made it home with my sanity intact.

She ended up cyber stalking me for a total of two years, at one point contacting my then girlfriend on social media with the objective of undermining the relationship. To say that she wreaked havoc with my life would be an understatement. On the positive side, she forced me to confront and address my simping. And for that I'm grateful I knew the bitch.

———————

"What an absolute she-devil," says the old man, grinning with amusement. "If you'd wanted to make your life a living hell, KitKat would've fit the bill. I bet she was good in bed—the crazy ones always are—but boy there would've been a price to pay for all that good pussy! Why, son, for the love of god, did you actively pursue a relationship with the whore?"

I shrug. "She was a fan of my work, and she went out of her way to contact me. There seemed to be something meaningful about the way we met. I figured, like she said, it was meant to be."

"That was superstitious of you!"

"I know that now. But—hold on—I thought you believed in spiritual stuff?"

"Ha! I believe in no such thing. I believe only in the natural world and the divine laws by which it is governed. Look, there's undoubtedly a kind of magic to how men and women come together to create a relationship. It's a delicate balance between opposites—yin and yang, sperm and ova, darkness and light, chaos and order. Whichever terms you wish to use appropriate to your respective belief system.

"We could dress it up in mystical language and speak

of alchemy and other things, but ultimately what we're referring to are the hidden and not so hidden factors that constitute human biology. The notion that it was 'meant to be' is fine if you're looking for a reason to justify how it is you ended up with one particular woman as opposed to another. Beyond that, it's bullshit."

"So you're saying there's no such thing as 'the one?' It's all meaningless?"

"There's no single 'one'; there are many potential 'ones.' And, no, it's not meaningless: you create the meaning for yourself. This means approaching relationships as tools for positive growth. A simp pedestalises women and relationships. He falls into the trap of thinking that, once he has a woman in his life, she'll become for him a source of infinite meaning and purpose. That's a tall, if not impossible, order. No woman, no matter how amazing and wonderful, can provide a man with the meaning and purpose he craves."

"What's the solution, then?"

"He must seek a higher purpose—one separate from yet complementary to his relationships with women. Men are uniquely compelled to venture out into the world in search of challenge and adventure—like the knights of old. Battles may be fought. Fire-breathing dragons may appear. And maybe, if he's lucky, he meets a beautiful maiden. Or, if not so lucky, an evil, seductive witch. Regardless of who or what he encounters on his path, he mustn't allow it to sway him from fulfilling his higher purpose."

"And what's his higher purpose?"

"That, son, I can't say: it's for each man to figure out for himself."

5

GIVE HER YOUR SHAFT, NOT YOUR BALLS

"You should move in," said Lucy. "I think it's time we took the leap."

I forced a smile. I wasn't sure what to say, so I figured it was best to stay silent. Hopefully she'd change the topic and we could get on with our evening. Maybe even have sex.

I'd been dating Lucy for six months now, and to move in together at this point, when we were still getting to know each other, struck me as foolish and risky. It was far too early in the relationship to take 'the leap.' Why was she so eager to rush things along?

"It's a big house," she continued. "You could have your own bedroom if you wanted."

"I'll think about it," I replied. "Forgot to ask: how was work today?"

Suddenly her eyes welled up with tears. "You're always stonewalling me! I'm so sick of this shit. I get the feeling you're not committed to this relationship!"

I took a deep breath. *'Keep calm, you can handle this,'* I kept telling myself. The last thing I wanted was another fight. I had to find a way to diffuse the situation.

I turned to face her fully, taking her hands in mine. "Look, I'm 100% committed to this relationship. I'd love to live with you one day, but my current place is cheap and I'm trying to save money right now. Besides, my lease doesn't end for another four months."

"You care more about money than our relationship. I never take priority in your life."

"That's not true, and you know it."

She was fully crying now, her face scrunched up like that of a child. Tears cascaded down her flushed cheeks. Nothing made my heart beat faster than seeing her cry and not knowing how to stop it. It was her habitual response when she failed to get her way. If I lived with her, I'd be trapped with the woman, forced to deal with her perpetual drama. The stress would probably kill me. Was there a fate worse?

I spent the next hour calming her down. I promised her that, as soon as my lease ended, we'd move in together. It was a lie, of course, but at least it put an end to the tears and prevented a nasty argument. She complained of a headache, so I made her a cup of camomile tea and gave her a chaste backrub before bed.

I hardly slept at all that night. I was angry, frustrated, agitated. The mattress felt hard and lumpy. The sound of Lucy's snoring didn't help. Mostly, though, it was my boner that was keeping me up. We hadn't had sex in over two weeks. She was continually coming up with excuses as to why she couldn't be intimate with me.

She kept saying she wanted to take the relationship to the next stage, beginning with us moving in together, but she wasn't exactly helping the process. If anything, she was driving a wedge between us with her damn crying and relentless theatrics. It was maddening. I was beginning to regret ever meeting the woman, let alone getting into a relationship with her.

———

The sad truth is that I didn't fully trust her. My trust in her was broken when, about two months into the relationship, I discovered she'd been lying about an important aspect of her past. Though I tried as best I could to convince myself of her trustworthiness, it was a band-aid solution at best. Trust isn't something you can fake. Either it's there or it isn't.

Lucy and I had met online. After more than a few negative experiences on *Tinder* and other dating apps, I'd made a promise to myself that I'd stay away from online dating and try to meet women in the real world instead. The convenience of online dating, however, was too enticing to resist. Simply put, I lacked the balls required to approach a woman directly and ask her out on a date.

I was impressed with Lucy's online dating profile. A former librarian from Queensland, she seemed refined, well-read, intelligent. Her responses to my questions were elegant and succinct. She looked pretty, too, with curly brown hair, large hazel eyes and a petite physique. She messaged me her number and we arranged a date via text. It almost seemed too easy.

On the morning of the date, she texted to inform me that she couldn't make it. She had dramatic news: she'd decided to move back to Queensland in search of work. This was a sudden decision, apparently, not something she'd planned in advance. It struck me as odd that someone would move interstate at the last moment. But I gave it little thought and wished her well.

Experience had taught me that, when a woman flakes on a date, it's generally an indication of low interest. Often such women are a lost cause. Sure, you can try to reschedule the date, though she's likely to give you the run-around. The golden rule is this: only bother with women who show high interest.

Lucy's level of interest was hard to gauge. I figured it was high because, several months after she moved to Queensland, she got back in touch with me and was keener than ever to chat. She worked several days a week as a disability support worker; the rest of the time she spent helping out her brother on his farm. Now that she was financially secure again, she was eager to move back to Tasmania. Life just wasn't the same in Queensland, she said. She missed the greenery and cooler climate of the Apple Isle.

Over the weeks that followed, Lucy and I got closer. Not physically closer—we lived thousands of miles apart—but emotionally closer, texting each other multiple times a day and spending many hours a week chatting online. Soon it developed into a sexual relationship, similar to what I'd had with KitKat.

Whereas KitKat was the kind of woman who tended to perform on camera, Lucy was more natural, less forced in the art of *Skype* sex. Not once did she struggle to come. Her usual routine was to straddle a pillow and ride it back and forth, her ample tits jiggling rhythmically in the process.

One night, having put my laptop away after a two-hour *Skype* session in which we'd both come multiple times, I was overcome by a sense of existential panic. I could feel myself becoming a simp again. Here I was engaged in another online, long-distance relationship with a woman. This time, at least, we lived in the same country. But was it not fundamentally the same relationship dynamic I'd created with KitKat?

I pushed such doubts aside. I told myself this relationship was different, better. It's not as though Lucy was some drug-fucked single mum who'd slept with sixty guys. While it's true she was sexually outgoing and had a "tramp stamp" (among other tattoos); and even though, judging from the stories she told of her past, she'd been a little wild in her twenties, I saw no evidence of rampant promiscuity. She drank in moderation and didn't take drugs. Yes, she'd been divorced twice. But divorces happen. I'd been divorced once. Was I any better?

During one of our evening *Skype* conversations, the topic of her sudden move to Queensland came up. "I can't believe you flaked on me," I joked, referring to the fact she'd cancelled on our date all those months ago.

I was getting a little suspicious at this point. There were things she'd told me about her brief time in Tasmania that didn't add up, all of which seemed to revolve around a guy named Gavin. Gavin had been her landlord at the time she lived in Tasmania. From him she'd rented a tiny cabin on a block of land in the forest.

Whenever she spoke about Gavin, her words were either extremely vague or accompanied by so many tears that it was impossible to discern much of value. I figured that, since we were now technically dating, I deserved a full explanation as to the nature of her relationship with Gavin. Had the two been dating? Were they friends with benefits?

After much prodding on my part, eventually she spilled the beans. "I didn't leave Tasmania for work reasons only. I left because Gavin was starting to get creepy, and I was worried my life was in danger.

"Holy shit," I said, unable to hide my astonishment. "What did he do?"

"I was renting a cabin from him, as you know. He seemed okay at first. A bit weird, but friendly. He kept coming over to fix things, even when they didn't need fixing. I'd come home from work, and he'd be there waiting for me. I told him I wasn't interested, but he persisted—buying me flowers, chocolates, asking me out on dates. One night I came home and he'd filled the bathtub with rose petals. He got stalkery, so I fled. I had to leave all of my stuff behind."

Gavin, it turned out, was only 23. A tall, blonde, extroverted, cocky electrician, he was the ultimate Chad. He spent his free time working out at the gym and was so proud of his rippling six-pack that he walked around shirtless whenever he came over to "fix" something. Lucy insisted, though, that she didn't find him attractive, not only because of the age difference (she was almost 40, old enough to be his mother) but mainly because of his "weird vibe." He struck her as "creepy," potentially even dangerous.

Lucy had tears streaming down her face as she related her experiences with Gavin, now and then pausing to dab her eyes with a tissue. She still suffered from post-traumatic stress disorder as a result of the ordeal, she claimed. Not yet was she out of the woods either. Lately Gavin had been sending her flirtatious emails and text messages. She was fearful that, if she moved back to Tasmania, there was a chance he'd find out and the stalking would continue.

I responded to Lucy's account with sympathy and understanding and promised I'd protect her from Gavin no matter what. Knowing how he'd treated her left me fuming in anger. What an absolute piece of shit,

I thought. How dare he scare and bully a defenceless woman!

Inside every simp there's a white knight ready to leap out to defend a woman from the cruel and tyrannical men who've done her wrong. It's satisfying to unleash your inner white knight. It makes you feel powerful and morally superior. Plus, women want to fuck guys who save them from abusive assholes, don't they?

A few days later, Lucy shared with me some exciting news: she'd applied for a job in Tasmania and was successful. In just a matter of weeks, she'd be packing up all of her possessions and moving down to Tasmania to live in the same town as me. We'd already met in person (I'd spent a week with her in Queensland) and while we'd hardly fallen in love, we'd felt enough of a connection to want to start dating. Finally, we'd get to enjoy a real relationship.

As Lucy was busy preparing to relocate, I began hatching what I considered a courageous plan. I would contact Gavin and request that he hand over to me the possessions belonging to Lucy that she'd left behind at his cabin. I figured it would bring a smile to her face and perhaps a sense of catharsis. Best of all, I'd get to be the hero.

When I told Lucy my plan, her reaction was mixed. Gavin, she warned me, was extremely possessive of her, jealous of other men in her life, and likely still bitter over the fact that she'd rejected his sexual advances. If I contacted him, there was a chance he'd lose his temper and threaten to beat me up. I assured her I'd be able to look after myself and told her not to worry. Eventually she caved in and gave me his number.

I called Gavin straight away. I was nervous to the point of nausea. He answered with a macho grunt and a testy "Who's this?"

I began by assuring him that I didn't want any trouble; that I only wanted to see Lucy's possessions returned to her. I asked him if there was somewhere we could meet—preferably in public—to arrange for this to happen.

"I'm not sure why you're calling me, mate," he replied, the tone of his voice conveying sincere perplexity. "Lucy and I are friends. We had an argument just before she left for Queensland, but that's behind us now."

"Really? She told me she left because you were harassing her.

He laughed, unimpressed. "No, mate, that's nonsense. Lucy's always saying stuff like that. She's a bit unstable, eh? She left because she couldn't pay the rent. Money troubles. Moving back to Queensland was my idea."

This was getting weird. It felt as though I'd entered an episode of the *Twilight Zone*. What the fuck was going on here? "So the two of you aren't on bad terms, then?"

More laughter. "No, mate. We had a bit of thing for a while. Nothing serious. She loves me, eh? She got upset when I told her I don't feel the same way. I'm bi, though I prefer guys. I told Lucy she needed to accept that, but I guess she's still disappointed with me."

My head was spinning at this point; I sat down on the edge of the bed. I didn't want to know more; I couldn't stomach it. I ended the call by telling Gavin to forget about returning Lucy's possessions. It was her problem, not mine. She'd lied to me. To hell with helping her.

I didn't call Lucy straight away; I needed a moment to settle my emotions. I wasn't so much angry with her as I was overcome by feelings of disappointment and betrayal. It left a sickening taste in my mouth. More than anything I was baffled. Why go to such lengths to conceal the fact that you've had a relationship with someone?

When I confronted her with Gavin's side of the story, she broke down crying and confessed that, indeed, she and Gavin had been close. Most evenings he'd drop by the cabin and they'd have dinner together and watch a movie. Occasionally he stayed the night, sleeping on the fold-out couch in the spare room. Yet, she insisted, theirs had never been a sexual relationship. They were simply good friends.

Good friends, really? Donning my detective's cap, I started going through the backlog of travel and lifestyle videos she'd posted on her *YouTube* channel, focusing on the ones she'd made in Tasmania. She and Gavin appeared together in several of the videos, the two flirting openly with each other and clearly having fun.

One video showed her and Gavin on holiday together at the beach, her dressed in a top showing ample cleavage and he sauntering around bare-chested, alpha Chad style. The most telling video of all, however, showed Lucy giving a tour of the cabin. It was tiny, with barely enough space to swing a cat. It featured neither a fold-out couch nor a spare room.

This concludes why, once Lucy arrived in Tasmania and we continued to see each other, I found myself unable to fully trust her. I accepted, of course, that she had a complex—and seemingly extensive—sexual past; and although it made me uncomfortable to know that she'd fucked a young Chad, I accepted that, too. What bothered me was the fact that she'd lied about it.

It was apparent she'd wanted to conceal the relationship owing to the significant age difference between her and her former lover and the judgment this was likely to attract from me and society at large. It appears there's nothing a woman fears more than loss of reputation.

Lucy and I dated, on and off, for about a year. Her betrayal hung over the relationship like a bad curse. Try as I might, I wasn't able to put it behind me. Lucy wasn't much help in this regard. Every now and then, as if to test me, she'd find a reason to bring up Gavin and my inability to accept her claim that they'd been "just friends" and not lovers.

She remained convinced that Gavin was trying, or would try, to stalk her. She at one point believed that he'd managed to access her smartphone remotely and was using it to track her movements. I chalked this up to paranoia on her part. There was no evidence to back up her claim, but rather every reason to believe that she was still besotted with the guy.

Lucy was a deeply strange woman, lacking, in my view, a stable sense of self. Identities she tried on like hats in a store. When I first met her, she was committed to progressive political causes and identified as a witch. Nine months later, she suddenly stopped being a witch and a progressive, transforming, literally overnight, into a Christian who opposed gay marriage.

One afternoon I visited her at her house to find that she'd thrown all of her pagan and occult paraphernalia—thousands of dollars' worth of crystals, Tarot cards and books—into a garbage bag on the floor. She'd come to believe the items were "cursed" and "satanic," she said. I watched as she hauled the devil's bag over her shoulder, walked out into the backyard, then dumped it into the garbage bin with a heavy clank.

I spent the next two hours seated beside her on the couch as she talked about freeing herself from "the dark powers." She looked completely different compared to the last time I saw her, and it wasn't just the shiny new crucifix around her neck. Her body language was more formal. She sat up straighter, smiled less, exhibited no trace of sexuality. Her sudden transformation she attributed to the power of the Holy Spirit.

Whereas I knew her before to be a naughty, witchy woman who enjoyed sucking my cock with the intensity of a vacuum cleaner (and who, no doubt, had sucked many cocks before mine) she was now a good Christian girl with impeccable morals and a holier-than-thou attitude. She bore almost no resemblance to the woman I'd chosen to date.

She wanted me to become a Christian, too, and, like a good little simp, I went along with it. I listened to her read entire chapters from the *Bible*; sat through documentaries about the lives of Jesus and the Saints (instead of the horror films we used to enjoy); and accompanied her to Sunday Mass. When she urged me to convert to Catholicism, I promised her I'd give it a try.

One afternoon at her house, Lucy sat me down and explained that, as a Christian, it was sinful of us to have sex out of wedlock. Thus, we were to cease all sexual activity immediately. Cuddles were okay, and maybe the occasional kiss, but a penis inside a vagina was a definite no-no. If I wanted to have sex with her, she said, I'd have to "earn it"—by marrying her.

I told Lucy I'd think about it. Of course, as she knew well, our relationship was on its last legs at this point; marriage was out of the question. By giving me an apparent choice between two unattractive alternatives— marriage or severe blue balls—she was placing me in an impossible situation in which I'd be compelled to choose neither. It was a manipulative tactic on her part to force me to end the relationship, allowing her to be the passive dumpee and not the guilt-ridden dumper.

Early the next day, I took a stroll down to the beach for a moment of solitude and quiet contemplation. It was cold, overcast, windy, the water bluish-green with a hint of grey. I stood with elbows resting on the rail of the boardwalk, watching the waves crash against the distant rocks.

What the fuck was I doing with my life? I wondered. If the woman I was currently dating lacked a stable identity, and if all of my exes were just as lost and damaged; what, precisely, did that say about me? How long could I afford to continue repeating these unhealthy cycles from the past?

Continuing to date Lucy when she no longer wanted to have sex with me was taking simping to a ridiculous level. It was pathetic. No, I wouldn't do it. I'd tell her the relationship was over. It's what she wanted anyway. Let her have her Catholicism and her celibacy. That was her choice, and to each their own, but it wasn't for me.

As I made my way back to the car, I made a promise to myself that I'd do whatever it takes to address and overcome my simping ways. I was tired of compromising, tired of grovelling, tired of making endless sacrifices for a woman. If I had to be alone, that was okay. It was time I forged my own path, with or without a woman in the picture. I would begin today, at this very moment.

From now on, I would stop simping and start living.

"Good for you," says the old man. How's it going so far?"

"Okay," I reply. "I no longer seek the attention and approval of women to the extent that I did before. Instead of making them the focus of my life, I put myself first."

He nods. "That's positive. What else?"

"I've been making an effort to be more honest with myself."

"How so?"

Laughing, I say, "By realising I'm not much healthier psychologically than the women I was involved with."

The old man smiles warmly in agreement. "Reminds me of a quote by a well-known therapist: 'We marry our unfinished business.' I'd say we also date our unfinished business, or seek them out." After a brief pause, he asks, "What was your childhood like? I assume it wasn't great."

Though it makes me uncomfortable to do so, I describe my childhood. I mention how, when I was only four, my parents separated. My mother, desiring her independence, moved away, leaving my father to assume the role of primary caregiver. With my mother largely out of the picture, I was starved of maternal warmth. As for my father, he cherished my older brother, but didn't feel much affection for me. I was therefore neglected by both parents and had no other choice but to raise myself.

"Sounds as though you suffered from a lack of love as a child," says the old man.

"That's an understatement."

"A lot of simps were unloved as children. Many of them come from fatherless homes and were raised by single mothers. The vast majority didn't get their needs met as children, in some cases because they were forced to provide emotional support to a dysfunctional parent—an alcoholic, for example. Such a child grows up starved of affection. He's left feeling inadequate, incomplete, defective, and unworthy of love. There's a hole inside of him that can't be filled. And so, as soon as he comes of age and gets into a relationship with a woman, the love he never received from his parents he tries to receive from her."

"Then what?"

"Very quickly the relationship deteriorates. A woman wants a man, not an insecure, grown up boy. Sensing there's a lack inside of him, that he isn't fully in his masculine element, she begins to act out in ways that destabilise the relationship. She does this subconsciously, for the most part, although some women do it wilfully, out of a desire to hurt and disrupt. She takes on the role of the dark, raging feminine. She becomes moody and distant. She continually nags and pushes his boundaries. She does this to test his strength, to see if he'll step up and be a man."

"And if he doesn't?"

"Then ultimately the relationship falls apart."

"What's the solution, then? How can a man with simping tendencies attract a high-quality woman into his life? And once he's managed to do so, how does he hold onto her?"

"Let's get something straight: one of the defining characteristics of being a simp is having few if any sexual or romantic options. Simps don't *attract* women. A simp settles for any woman who'll take him. If he was able to attract a woman, it would mean he has options. Options imply power and autonomy—qualities antithetical to the very notion of simping. Therefore, any woman he might attract would undoubtedly be of higher quality than the kind of woman he'd normally end up with. She'd likely stick around, too, *if* he managed to work on himself and not give into his simping tendencies.

"To answer a simplified version of your question,

he attracts a woman into his life by not overly desiring one in the first place. It's paradoxical, I know, but bear in mind that women are paradoxical creatures. They don't think or operate the same way as us."

"In other words, treat 'em mean keep 'em keen?"

The old man smiles and rolls his eyes. "No, I don't advise acting like a jerk, although it's true that plenty of women are attracted to bad boys. I'm referring to the opposite: complete honesty and authenticity. This requires the cultivation of a certain mindset. A man with this mindset knows, deep down, that he doesn't need a woman to complete him. He'll graciously walk away from a woman and not look back if she ceases to add value to his life. Though he'd prefer to be in a relationship with a good woman—he has too much self-respect to settle for a bad or even mediocre one—being alone doesn't bother him. Either way, he's content with his lot."

"That's very stoic! I think I understand what you mean. It's an attitude of self-reliance and non-neediness."

"Exactly. These are typically masculine qualities. As are strength, leadership, bravery, stability, and trustworthiness. When a woman encounters a man who has these qualities in spades, she can't help but feel a strong pull of attraction to him. She wants to receive the gifts that he, as a high-quality man, is uniquely able to provide. She wants to be filled—and, yes, that includes being filled by his cock.

"Of course, the masculine and the feminine have very different roles and attributes; the feminine is receptive, passive and nurturing, whereas the masculine seeks to conquer, penetrate, expand, and—most important of all—give."

Suddenly it makes sense. My desire to have a woman in my life has long originated from a place of neediness. And, yet, as a man, my role is to give rather than receive. It's time I flipped the script.

"I can promise you," continues the old man, "once you're able to approach relationships from the standpoint of what you can give to a woman, selflessly, bravely, lovingly, without expecting anything in return and without compromising your values and integrity in the process, your problem won't be failing to attract women. Your problem will be attracting so many that you'll have to push some of them away. Speaking of which, we've reached the end of this discussion and it's time you left me in peace."

And with that I thank the old man, wish him goodbye, and start on my journey home.

EPILOGUE

I met the woman of my dreams outside a fish and chip shop situated near the beach, against the backdrop of a golden-pink sunset, while Tom Petty's *I Won't Back Down* played in the background.

It was a chance encounter, the kind that only happens in a Hollywood movie. I'd been walking by, lost in my own internal world, when I heard a feminine voice say, "Cool hat."

I stopped, turned, and there she was: a beautiful creature with sea green eyes and fiery red hair. She sat reclined on one of the many benches that overlooked the shorefront. Hers was a pear-shaped physique: wide hips, a slim waist, prominent thighs, and breasts large but not overly so. I couldn't see her ass directly on account of her being seated. Yet, as a connoisseur of the booty, I had sufficient visual data to assume that her trunk was not lacking for junk.

I blinked a few times, adjusted my glasses with my

thumb and index finger. "What did you say?" I asked, still not quite believing that she'd spoken to me and not someone else.

She smiled, apparently flirting. "I said I like your hat. Reminds me of *Peaky Blinders*."

"Thanks," I replied. "It's called a flat cap."

"It's cool. Much better than the baseball caps I see a lot of guys wearing."

"I like your style too," I said, referring to her brown leather boots, Demin overalls and a white tee-shirt. I'm not normally a fan of overalls on a woman—it's a style of attire popular among radical feminists and butch lesbians—but exceptions exist and here was living proof. "So what brings you here on this sunny afternoon?"

She ignored my question and instead introduced herself. Her name was Angela. She was a first-year medical science student who'd recently moved to the area to study at the local university. I placed her age at roughly twenty-five.

It quickly became apparent that she wasn't interested in small talk. She preferred to discuss bigger topics. Over the next hour, she spoke with passion and eloquence about her interest in the human body, focusing on evolutionary biology.

She wasn't, like a lot of young women these days, some rampant social justice warrior who believed gender to be a social construct. Rather, to my relief, she expressed the view that men and women are fundamentally different, serving distinct but complementary roles.

This was my kind of woman: smart, well-spoken, passionate about her interests, and independent-minded enough to not buy into the propaganda of the times. Before we parted ways, I asked her for her number, suggesting we go out for a drink sometime. She gave it to me without hesitation.

Our first date led to a second date. Then a third. Soon we started dating officially. I'm pleased to say that we're now a couple and the relationship is going wonderfully. Our conversations are always effortless and stimulating. She's an excellent cook, amazing in bed, and, best of all, I feel secure enough in the relationship to not slip into simp mode.

No, I lie. We aren't dating. After that encounter, I never saw her again. When I asked her for her number, she instead offered to send me a *Facebook* friend request, taking out her phone to do so. Once home, I noticed that the request, though sent, had immediately been cancelled. She'd given me the *Facebook* equivalent of a fake number. She'd deceived me, rejected me. Fuck.

I should add that the conversation didn't go as smoothly as described. Overcome by anxiety, I started fidgeting, repeatedly placing my hands in the pockets of my jeans. I was unable to stand still, my knees trembling a little. I became tongue-tied, failing to project my voice with clarity and confidence.

Furthermore, I allowed the conversation to drag on too long. By the time it came to an end, the sun had set and it was rapidly growing dark. The fish and chip shop had shut its doors, the music was no longer playing, and there was no one around but us. Angela, suddenly aware of the lateness of the hour and the fact that we were alone, stood up with a startled expression on her face.

"Would you like me to walk you back to the campus?" I mumbled, taking a step back to give her some space. This only compounded her unease. She declined with a shake of her head, scurrying off down the path in the exact opposite direction to the campus building.

For days following the encounter, I felt like a pathetic loser. An attractive and intelligent young woman
had struck up a conversation with me and I'd handled
it poorly, making every simp mistake in the book. I'd
come across as needy, desperate, awkward. Keen to
date her, I'd badly wanted her to like me. Worse, I'd left
her feeling anxious and unable to trust me, so much so
that she'd literally fled.

For the last two years I've been seeing a therapist. He's
a portly, chronically sarcastic Scotsman in his late-40s
who for years worked as an industrial engineer before
realising that his true calling lay in the treatment of
mental health. His clients have included paedophiles
and hardened criminals. The vast majority are ordi-
nary people like myself who struggle in their lives for
one reason or another.

Decent therapists are as rare as hen's teeth. Most
are awful. Mine is one of the better ones. We don't
see eye-to-eye on everything, nor should we. Your
therapist isn't your friend. A therapist worth their salt
will be able to identify your shit and call you out on it,
prompting you to take action to change for the better.

My therapist knows I'm a simp. My difficulties with
women we've spoken about extensively, particularly
within the context of social anxiety—an issue I've
struggled with since my teens.

My chief problem, as revealed by therapy, could be
summed up as follows: I believe deep down that I'm not
good enough as I am; that I'm defective, inadequate,
flawed, unloved and unlovable. In short, I operate under a negative and distorted self-image. Consequently,
I approach social interactions—with women especial-

ly—from the standpoint of one who is lacking. There's a voice in my head that continually shouts: *You suck, buddy!*

When I next met up with my therapist, I described to him my encounter with Angela and how it left me feeling worthless and humiliated. "I feel terrible about it," I said. "She literally ran off! She probably thought I was a creep. What if I run into her at again? How should I act? What should I say?"

With his brows furrowed, he swiped the air as if to say "shush," the way he always does when I'm over-complicating a situation. "It's a small town, sure, but chances are you'll never see her again. And if you do bump into each other, so what? It's not as though her world revolves around you, you know."

"What do you mean?"

"That you're not the centre of her universe, Chuck. She has her own life going on, her own problems. You were probably one of many males she spoke to that night. Maybe she was mistreated by an ex-boyfriend. Maybe she already has a boyfriend. Or maybe she's tired of guys always wanting something from her. In the final analysis, her reaction says more about her than it does about you."

I shrugged. "I suppose. So I didn't do anything wrong, then?"

He stood up and, with hands clasped together as if in prayer, began pacing back and forth in front of me, thinking deeply. It was at least ten seconds before he finally spoke.

"You did nothing wrong, no. But there is—how should I put it?—room for improvement. You stood there talking to her for over an hour. You need to know when to hit the eject button, and that goes for any conversation. There was probably a moment initially where she felt connected to you. Then, as the conversation dragged on, that ceased to be. Relationships are fundamentally about connection, yes?"

I lowered my head in disappointment and self-loathing. "For once I meet a woman who actually likes me and somehow I find a way to screw it up."

"There's a more constructive way to look at it, Chuck. How you're perceived by others is largely within your control. It involves how you carry yourself. What you say. How you say it."

"I know, my social skills are awful, especially with women."

"They could do with some polishing, sure. But you haven't let me finish my point. How you're perceived by others is only one half of the equation. The other, more important half is how you perceive yourself—which at present is overly critical. What Angela thought of you, what others think of you, isn't worth losing sleep over. You need to accept yourself as you are. Eventually you'll meet someone who likes you *for you*. Don't forget the golden rule: relationships are about connection."

With obvious sarcasm, I asked, "So it's okay if I turn up to work with no pants?"

"Sure."

"Really?"

He chuckled. "Well, I do recommend wearing pants to work. Mind you, there are cultures where men don't wear pants. Take the kilt, for example. Perfectly acceptable in Scotland, though not so common over here."

"Do you wear a kilt?"

"Er, no. I don't. I don't play the bagpipes either. The point I was trying to make is that social interactions are context specific and highly nuanced. When you make sweeping generalisations about women, such as 'all women are like this,' or 'women don't like me for reason X or Y,' you do yourself a disservice. You limit your thinking. What's considered attractive to one woman may not be considered attractive to another. Do you get my point?"

"I get your point, though I'm not sure if it helps."

"Why not?"

"Because it doesn't change the fact that, thanks to feminism, society as a whole is hostile towards men."

"Feminism has its relevance, Chuck. Women have been oppressed and abused by men for millennia, although now the pendulum's swung a little too far in the opposite direction, which has made things, er...a bit challenging for men. There are plenty of good women out there, though, and they're all unique. There are artistic, creative women. Outgoing women who flock to pubs and rock concerts. Sporty women. Geeky women who dress up in costumes and attend comic conventions. I could go on."

"I get what you're saying: don't change yourself to suit other people. Be yourself. Seek out your own tribe. That sort of thing."

"That's the gist of it, yes. As for societal and political factors over which you have no control—such as feminism—they're important to recognise, too. The struggles you've had in your relationships with women—and with what you call 'simping'—are far too common among my male clients. Your problem isn't rare or unique. Nothing happens in a microcosm, Chuck. Be sure to remember that."

"I don't get it," I asked, genuinely confused.

He sighed. "Occasionally I'm forced to be deliberately vague so that I don't lose my job. Let me explain it another way: it's not always you that's the problem. Sometimes society is in large part to blame."

Just as alcoholism is for life, so too is simping. An alcoholic may sign up with Alcoholics Anonymous and henceforth refuse to touch another drop of booze, yet their weakness for alcohol will remain with them till the grave, necessitating ongoing support from others who recognise their plight. The same goes for simping. The best one can hope for—and I speak from experience—is gradual improvement, day by day, preferably done under the guidance of a licensed therapist and with continual input from male friends and mentors. I'm pleased to say that I'm less of a simp now than I was, say, a year ago. If this trend continues it means I'm doing well.

As a man starts to recover from simping, what he previously perceived as negative and humiliating experiences with women become opportunities for growth and learning. Whereas, a couple of years ago, being "rejected" by Angela would've left me feeling bummed out for a week, I instead got over it in a few days. With my therapist's prompting, I used it as an opportunity to recognise where I'd gone wrong and thus improve how I relate to and communicate with women.

I've put quotes around the term "rejected" for a reason. When a woman fails to give me her number or says "no" to a date, no longer do I consider myself rejected by her. The term "rejected" is negative and unhelpful; it doesn't serve me, but in fact brings me down. More important, it's neither a factual nor honest way of looking at the situation. Rejection is a judgement, not a fact. We're only rejected by others in so far as we judge ourselves to be rejected by them. Nowadays I frame rejection as follows: *I was turned down by a woman due to lack of mutual interest.*

It behoves us to be precise with the language we employ when communicating with ourselves and others, because language is the medium of story, and it's through stories that we contextualise and define our everyday experience. Not only do these stories shape our experience of reality, they *are* our reality. Fortunately, by being skilled and discerning users of language, we can construct better stories, ones that promote growth and learning rather than negativity and narrow-mindedness.

Here, for example, is the story I initially told myself about Angela:

I met an attractive woman, a goddess, but I fucked it up and she rejected me. No doubt she thought of me as a complete loser. Now I'm destined to be alone for the rest of my pathetic existence.

And here's the reframed version:

Today while going for my evening walk, a young woman engaged me in conversation. She was in a talkative, open mood. Though I perceived her behaviour as flirtatious, it's possible she simply wanted to chat to someone and I happened to be walking by at the right moment.

Overwhelmed by her physical attractiveness, I allowed my imagination to run away with me. I began to picture what it would be like to date and sleep with her. She became for me an object of desire and attachment. Fixated on the goal of making her my girlfriend, I lost touch with the magic of the present moment. I was convinced that, in order to succeed in my mission, I had to make her like me. To this end, I tried my best to say the 'right' things and act the 'right' way. I felt it would be a sure path to rejection to allow her to see the real me. This prompted me to feel self-conscious and anxious.

Despite the lateness of the hour and the fact that the conversation was dragging, I stuck around, unable to give up on the goal of making her my girlfriend. Like the song playing in the background, I refused to "back down." There was little connection between us at this point, which is why, upon asking her out on a date, she declined—albeit indirectly. Not that it matters. It was an experience from which I can learn.

Next time I have a conversation with an attractive woman, I'll try to remain focused on the present moment and simply enjoy the process of getting to know her.

As you can see, the latter narrative is more accurate in content and far more positive in tone than the former. This technique of reframing an experience is the cornerstone of cognitive behavioural therapy (CBT), by means of which harmful and distorted patterns of thinking are held up to the light of reality, found to be false, and so replaced by healthier, more accurate patterns of thinking. It can have a profoundly positive impact on one's mental health.

Stoicism, a school of philosophy that originated in Greece around 300 BC, was the inspiration for modern CBT. Thousands of years before psychology as a field of science emerged, the stoics recognised that between our impressions (thoughts, perceptions, etc.) and the resultant feelings and reactions are judgments. "It isn't the events themselves that disturb people, but only their judgements about them," to quote the Stoic philosopher Epictetus. Judgments, when handled poorly, are the source of much suffering among human beings. Fortunately, we have the freedom to choose how we form our judgements.

Let's say that while walking to work one morning you bump into an acquaintance whom you last saw three years ago, named Greg. Pleased to see him, you smile and say hello. Your immediate expectation is that he'll smile back and stop to catch up on old times. Looking perturbed and rushed, he responds with a curt nod and continues on his way.

This brief interaction could be labelled an impression (though in truth it consists of multiple impressions). From this impression arises a judgement. You decide that Greg was perturbed because of you; worst still, that he no longer likes you, and perhaps never liked you to begin with. These negative thoughts prompt other negative thoughts, creating a snowball of pessimism that lasts throughout the day.

If, on the other hand, you were a practicing Stoic, you would approach the situation differently. Staying cool, calm and collected, you would choose to adopt a very different judgment: that Greg's mood had nothing to do with you. After all, people have their own problems; and you have no idea what's going on in Greg's life, especially since you haven't seen him in years. You shrug your shoulders and continue on with your day.

The conclusion is simple but not always obvious: how we choose to interpret events affects how we perceive ourselves and the world around us, which in turn impacts the quality of our life. This process continues on in the manner of a feedback loop.

There is a further insight to be gleaned here; one that concerns attention and the management thereof. Attention, when harnessed and utilised effectively, is a tremendous source of power. Power is the ability to act or have influence over ourselves, our situation, and other people. While having influence over others is not in itself a bad thing (it depends *how* you influence others), in this instance I'm using the term in a personal sense, to refer to an attitude or state of mind.

You exercise your personal power when you set a goal for yourself and achieve it, or when you take responsibility for your actions, thoughts, decisions and preferences, without being swayed and influenced by others. Personal power implies sovereignty. It means to be the master of your fate and the captain of your soul, to paraphrase a certain famous poem. Personal power is the very thing that simps and nice guys lack, and which they therefore need to cultivate and reclaim.

Throughout each day, particularly in our dealings with other people, demands are made upon our attention. Depending on how we manage these demands, we either preserve our personal power or allow it to be compromised and stolen from us. If we're highly agreeable, the latter tends to happen more often than the former.

Let's say you work with an annoying colleague who enjoys banal conversation and gossip. We'll call him Steve. Every time you try to focus and get some work done, Steve immediately starts talking at you. These one-way conversations can last thirty minutes and they not only bore you but significantly undermine your productivity.

You could tell Steve you're busy and unable to make chit chat. Conversely—and this is what a simp or nice guy would do—you could stop what you're doing and give him your complete and undivided attention, silently dying inside while he drones on about the price of nails at the hardware store.

In the former case, you're retaining your personal power and maintaining healthy boundaries. You're putting yourself first and choosing to be assertive. In the latter, you're being overly agreeable and allowing yourself to be treated as a doormat. You're indicating that your time, energy and attention doesn't matter, and that ultimately you're not worth much as a person.

Attention is a finite resource; there's only so much of it we can give, and only so many things we can give it to, at any particular moment. To our detriment, we live in a society that increasingly makes demands upon our attention. Ours is a heavily digital age in which our lives are spent partly in the real world and partly in the virtual world; to occupy both is attention consuming indeed.

Social media, video games, dating apps, streaming services such as *Netflix*, and of course pornography—all are purposely designed to consume our attention for the sake of turning a profit, providing little of value to the consumer except for momentary pleasure and the chance to escape reality.

Due to the increasingly ubiquitous nature of the digital world, the attraction to renounce our attention and therefore power has never been stronger. Throughout the course of the day, moments arise where, feeling bored, I find myself tempted to watch another *YouTube* video or check my social media feed. These moments compel me to reflect and ask, 'Shall I be strong or shall I be a simp?'

Though we fail to see it, there is a war going on for our minds. The architects of this war aren't shape-shifting lizard people from Nibiru, but rather men and women who dress in expensive suits and work in brightly-lit, air-conditioned offices. Like us, they go by names like Olivia and David and their guilty pleasures include bad pop music, fast food, and the occasional wank in the shower. They're only exceptional in so far as they're shockingly intelligent and not weighed down by empathy and a moral code. They are high-functioning sociopaths.

From their perspective, we who make up the masses are little more than rats in a laboratory experiment made to crawl through mazes for food pellet rewards. Unlike in a laboratory setting, however, there is no need for scalpels and other crude instruments. The tools and techniques they employ are primarily psychological. In fact, much social engineering takes place within the domain of marketing, the currency of which is attention. To know something about the principles of marketing is to possess an understanding of how society is shaped and manipulated by means of social engineering programs—some dating back centuries and executed over multiple generations.

Advertising, a component of marketing, explicitly reveals how attention, once captured, can be easily converted into dollars. An effective advertisement will capture your attention so completely that you end up handing over your hard-earned cash for the product or service advertised. Gillette razors, anyone? The best a man can get?

Simping, as explained, isn't exclusively an individual problem. "Nothing happens in a vacuum," to requote my therapist. While, in this present book, my focus has been to explore simping from an individual perspective, I'd be a very slack writer indeed if I didn't at least touch on the socio-political side of the phenomenon.

Men—particularly white heterosexual men—are currently the target of a sophisticated, multi-faceted social engineering and psychological warfare campaign that (1) aims to weaken and feminise the male population and strip men of their power, in part by undermining the very concept of masculinity by labelling it "toxic"; and (2) pit men and women against each other, thus fuelling a "gender war" that, among other things, is destabilising the traditional nuclear family unit, while encouraging singledom and rampant promiscuity.

The ultimate goal of this project is to usher in a female-centric social order, a matriarchy—something that, while presented as empowering to women, will ultimately have the exact opposite effect, since there are no winners in this game. Indeed, the proliferation of miserable cat ladies who spend their days drinking cask wine and watching daytime television is proof that the increasing feminisation of society is just as detrimental to women as it is men.

That the game is rigged and devoid of winners is something that bears repeating. While men and women are being played against each other, by means of the age-old tactic of divide and conquer, society is being gradually usurped not by Big Brother but by something equally terrifying: Big Mother.

The Big Mother agenda is insidious, far-reaching and impossible to avoid. Nowadays, a boy raised in the West will grow up believing he's part of the "evil patriarchy," that men are naturally violent and sexually aggressive, and consequently to express—let alone embrace—his masculinity is to commit an act of violence.

In school, the majority of his teachers will be female. At home it'll be mum who wears the pants. Either he'll have a submissive, emotionally absent father or no father to speak of. Though he'll long for a positive male role model to emulate and look up to, his chance of finding one—either in the real world or in the world of pop culture—will be virtually nil. By the time he reaches his teens, he'll be deeply confused about his identity and what it means to be a man. Unable to acquire a girlfriend, he'll spend many hours a week jerking off to scenes on his computer that do not constitute normal or healthy expressions of human sexuality, further weakening his spirit and setting him firmly on the path to simphood.

I could go on, though my point is clear: young males are being conditioned and manipulated in such a way that their chance of developing into strong, healthy men is compromised from the beginning. Grown up boys addicted to porn, video games, woke *Marvel* movies and strawberry flavoured soy milk, who lack responsibility, purpose and a clear direction in life, and who feel deeply ashamed about their very maleness, are hardly a threat to the establishment. Which, of course, is the point: to allow the sisterhood to rise up and take the reins of society, you must first weaken and atomise the male population.

In my case, while growing up in the eighties and nineties, it wasn't only pornography but also Hollywood films featuring young male protagonists that exerted the strongest influence in terms of shaping me into a simp. The overriding message of these films was as follows: romantic love is of ultimate value; to have a woman in your life will bring you everlasting happiness. However, since women appreciate nice, sensitive guys, make sure you don't do anything that might cause you to be perceived as a jerk. Oh, and once you get a girlfriend, you must, to keep her happy, sacrifice everything for her and make her the centre of your universe. Have a good life, dipshit!

Simping, regardless of the form it takes or the scale on which it occurs, comes back to the notion of power. While simping on a societal level could be thought of as the process by which men are being collectively weakened, feminised and encouraged to hand over their power to the sisterhood to make way for the emergence of a female-centric society, simping on an individual level involves giving your power away to a woman by placing her on a pedestal and making her the arbiter of your self-worth, with the objective of gaining sex and affection in return.

Of course, it isn't all doom and gloom. Simping is done voluntarily, not by force, and there exist practical ways to curtail it. The process of healing begins on an individual level, by practicing self-discipline and mindfulness. At each moment in your life, you have the option to decide to whom or what you give your attention and therefore power.

To curtail my own simping tendencies, I now follow a set of rules that pertain to how I conduct myself around women. If, after expressing romantic interest in a woman, my advances aren't immediately reciprocated, I instantly walk away and stop wasting my time; I cease messaging or talking to her. Furthermore, I no longer do favours for women just because I find them attractive or because I expect to gain something in return. I try, as best I can, to treat all women equally— young, old, attractive, unattractive. So far these rules have held me in good stead.

Although the overwhelming focus of this book is on women, and how, by being a simp, relationships with women can go terribly wrong, the main message I wish to convey is one of personal empowerment and self-improvement. As I've hopefully made clear in these pages, there is more to life than women and relationships. If, as a man, you go through life thinking that a woman will complete you, or magically make your life better, then you're setting yourself up for misery and disappointment.

There is much discussion on the internet among advocates of MGTOW (men going their own way) and red pill philosophy, particularly on *YouTube*, as to what constitutes for a man a worthy life purpose. This content, taken as a whole, overwhelmingly conveys a message of self-improvement by means of acquiring wealth, status, and muscles, so as to eventually attain the pinnacle of "alpha."

In much the same way that, according to the Buddhists, "enlightenment" is the answer to overcoming suffering, embodying "alphaness," we're told, is the answer to becoming a complete and liberated man. Once you're an alpha superman with a rippling six-pack, a swinging dick and a bank account brimming with "fuck you" money, women will be drawn to you like iron filings to a magnet and you won't lack for pussy ever, apparently. Or much of anything else.

I think this is nonsense, and it's not because I'm about as far from alpha as a cat is from being a turtle, never mind the ambiguity of what "alpha" means exactly. If you want to aspire to be alpha, that's fine. To each their own. From my perspective, though, it's a superficial goal. I believe, like the Stoics of old, that gaining tranquillity, virtue and wisdom has far greater value as an accomplishment than the acquisition of bling, pussy and fast cars under the guise of masculinity and alphaness.

I suspect that some who read this book will label me a misogynist and criticise me for "hating on" women. That I have something against women is patently untrue. If anything, I criticise men, including myself, far more harshly than I do women. If it appears that I stereotype women (and, to a lesser extent, men), it's not intentional; it's because I'm of the opinion that men and women are, by nature, worlds apart.

I don't believe men are superior to women nor women superior to men. To suggest as much would be simple-minded and absurd. We're simply different, two sides of the one coin that is the species Homo sapiens. Just as the back of a coin can never perceive the front, so it's impossible for men and women to fully understand one another. Never the twain shall meet, and that's as nature intended it.

Yet there lies deep within us the desire to comprehend the thoughts and motives of the opposite sex. People do this when they engage in idle gossip and speculation about "this girl I met at the bar" or "that guy at work who's always giving me the eye." Is it not more constructive to go about this consciously rather than unconsciously, even if, in the former case, it entails examining those aspects of male and female nature that are likely to provoke discomfort and controversy?

Nowadays, when I find myself in the company of one or more attractive women, I try to use it as an opportunity for personal growth, and to learn more about female nature. I enter into this process with a spirit of curiosity and a desire to learn, much like a scientist gathering data. I'm always surprised and sometimes a little disturbed by what I discover about myself—and the opposite sex—during these exercises.

Recently, I was invited to a small religious gathering consisting of men and women in their mid to early twenties. Present was a young woman with Mediterranean features—full lips, a delicate nose, curly brown hair and olive skin. She reminded me of a girl I'd once had a crush on in high school. Observing her from across the room as she spoke to a friend, I found myself assessing her availability as a potential partner. As far as I could tell she was single; there was no boyfriend present.

The moment she was alone, I gingerly approached her and introduced myself. As we exchanged small talk, I observed myself with the detachment of a spectator as, automatically, the simp part of me rose to the fore. This took expression in my body language and speech. I nodded enthusiastically to her comments, laughed on cue. I leaned forward, listening with bated breath to everything she said. It was almost as if mentally and to some extent physically, I was *wrapping myself around her*.

An interesting realisation occurred during this moment, not limited to the mental "wrapping" described above. I was projecting my attention towards her, and in the process depleting the awareness in my body. In fact, I could no longer feel my body; it had become numb. I may as well have been an empty shell.

With mindfulness comes the ability to effect change. The solution, I realised, was to come back to my body, to fill it with awareness. This I achieved by taking deep breaths from my diaphragm and exhaling slowly. Very soon I was back in my body and as a result my anxiety diminished. Feeling centred and in control, I was able to perceive her as her own unique person, rather than through the needy, objectifying eyes of a simp.

I quickly determined that she wasn't the least bit attracted to me. This I had no issue with. To my surprise, I realised I wasn't attracted to her either; I'd been led astray by the simp within. Although on a purely physical level she had many appealing features, there was nothing about her essence to which I felt drawn. We were incompatible, cheese and chalk. Yet whereas she'd been aware of our lack of chemistry early on in the interaction, I'd been slow on the uptake.

Later that night, I retired to bed feeling not as though I'd been rejected by an attractive woman, but as though I'd been given a profound gift. For the first time I realised in a very real, practical sense that the antidote to simping, as with most problems of the psyche, can be found in the greatest of all Ancient Greek aphorisms: "Know thyself."

ABOUT THE AUTHOR

CHUCK VALENTINE is an Australian author whose work focuses on self-development and positive masculinity. A recovering simp who wasted much of his youth pedestalising and pleasing women, he's now focused on leading a life of purpose, passion and meaning. He tidies his room every day and visits the gym four times a week. And though he's still an occasional sucker for the booty, he remains committed to his life's purpose: to inspire other men to stop simping and start living.

www.ingramcontent.com/pod-product-compliance
Lightning Source LLC
Chambersburg PA
CBHW032353280326
41935CB00008B/559